BOLA AKIN-JOHN

The
Matured
Pastor's
Wife
&
Female
Minister

**Becoming The Noble Woman
God Created You To Be.**

PUBLISHED BY

CHURCH GROWTH SERVICES INC.
BLOCK C, FHA ABESAN IV ESTATE, CF STREET,
OFF CA STREET, MOSAN B/STOP, IPAJA, LAGOS.
P. O. BOX 3747, OSHODI, LAGOS.
TEL: +234-1-8976100, 08023000714, 08029744296
E-MAIL- AKINGROW@YAHOO.COM
WEBSITE: WWW.CHURCHGROWTHAFRICA.ORG

PRINTED IN NIGERIA BY:
LIFE & MINISTRY PUBLICATIONS
TEL.: 234-1-7934133, (O)8037152451

CONTENTS

4

DEDICATION

I LOVINGLY DEDICATE THIS BOOK TO
PASTOR MRS. FOLU ADEBOYE.
WHO HAS PROVED OVER THE YEARS THAT
SHE IS A MATURED PASTOR'S WIFE
IN ALL RAMIFICATIONS.
MAY GOD CONTINUE TO STRENGTHEN YOU M.

6

APPRECIATION

WRITING A BOOK ON THIS TITLE WOULDN'T HAVE BEEN EASY, BEING A MAN, IF NOT FOR THE HOLY SPIRIT. THEREFORE, MY SPECIAL APPRECIATION TO HIM FOR THE UNIQUE INSPIRATION HE GAVE ME TO SUCCESSFULLY WRITE THIS BOOK.

SPECIAL THANKS TO MY WIFE, KEMI, FOR YIELDING HERSELF TO GOD FOR GROWTH AND MATURITY IN HER LIFE AND MINISTRY OVER THE YEARS. YOUR LIFE IS A GOOD FRAME WORK FOR 'THE MATURED PASTOR'S WIFE AND FEMALE MINISTER'. KEEP YIELDING TO HIM MY LOVE.

MY ASSOCIATES AND STAFF HAVE BEEN SPECIAL. MICHAEL OLUWANIYI, ELIJAH

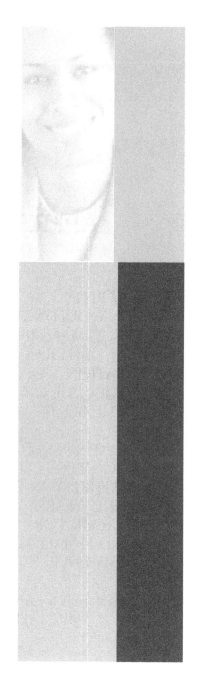

8

INTRODUCTION

I BELIEVE THAT THIS IS A LONG OVERDUE BOOK. YES, I HAVE COME ACROSS SOME BOOKS THAT ADDRESS THE MINISTERS' WIVES, BUT THEY ARE FEW AND THEY LARGELY FAILED TO ADDRESS THE SALIENT ISSUES CONFRONTING THE WIFE OF GOSPEL MINISTERS TODAY AND FEMALE MINISTERS. OVER THE YEARS THERE HAD BEEN LOTS OF WOMEN CONFERENCES HERE AND THERE, BUT THEY HAVE LARGELY FAILED TO PROFFER SOLUTIONS TO THE MYRIADS OF CHALLENGES CONFRONTING THE PASTORS' WIVES AND FEMALE MINISTERS DAILY.

THE MAIN REASON FOR WRITING THIS BOOK IS TO CONFRONT HEADLONG, THE MANY ISSUES THAT ARE DAILY POSING SERIOUS CHALLENGES TO THE AVERAGE PASTORS'

WIVES. OVER THE YEARS GOD HAS OPPORTUNED ME TO SHARE WITH AND EMPOWER PASTORS TO DO A BETTER JOB OF LEADING THE CHURCH IN A HEALTHY WAY. AND THAT HAS MADE ME TO COME IN CONTACT WITH MANY WIVES OF PASTORS, MINISTERS AND LADY MINISTERS. I HAVE SEEN THE GOOD, THE BAD AND THE UGLY. I HAVE SEEN THE INCREDIBLE DAMAGES THAT CARELESS MINISTERS' WIVES CAN DO TO THEMSELVES, THEIR HUSBANDS, MINISTRIES AND THE BODY OF CHRIST.

DURING THE TSUNAMI DISASTER OF 2004, IN WHICH OVER 300,000 LIVES WERE LOST IN SOUTH EAST ASIA, AN INCREDIBLE STORY CAME OUT OF IT. IT WAS THE STORY OF A LITTLE CHURCH OVER A SMALL HILL. AS THE TSUNAMI WAS COMING, DESTROYING EVERYTHING IN ITS PATH, THE SMALL CONGREGATION GATHERED OUTSIDE THE CHURCH AS DESTRUCTION APPROACHED. THEY LOOKED UP TO THE PASTOR AND HE TOLD THEM THAT THEY SHOULD GO INSIDE THE CHURCH AND START TO CRY TO GOD. THEY ALL OBEYED AND WENT INSIDE THE CHURCH. AFTER SOME MINUTES OF PRAYING, THE PASTOR'S WIFE STOOD UP, PICKED HER DAUGHTER AND RAN OUT OF THE CHURCH IN FEAR AND UNBELIEF. THE OTHER CHURCH MEMBERS CONTINUED TO PRAY WITH THE PASTOR. AFTER SEVERAL MINUTES, THEY STOPPED AND WENT OUTSIDE. TO THEIR AMAZEMENT, THE TSUNAMI HAD PASSED THEM OVER. EVERYTHING IN SIGHT FOR MILES WERE DESTROYED, ONLY THE SMALL CHURCH BUILDING REMAINED STANDING. THE PASTOR'S WIFE AND DAUGHTER WERE NEVER SEEN AGAIN.

UNFORTUNATELY, TOO MANY WIVES OF PASTORS FALL INTO THIS TRUE LIFE STORY TODAY. THEY DON'T BELIEVE THE CALL AND ANOINTING UPON THEIR HUSBANDS AND THEY ARE PAYING HEAVY PRICE FOR THEIR UNBELIEF. I HAVE COME TO UNDERSTAND THREE FACTS IN THIS MATTER:-

1. LOTS OF PASTORS' WIVES ARE STRUGGLING

YES, MANY WOMEN DID NOT MARRY THEIR HUSBANDS AS PASTORS AND GOSPEL MINISTERS. THEY MARRIED THEM AS UNBELIEVERS OR ORDINARY CHRISTIANS AND WHEN THEY BECAME PASTORS, IT BECAME A BIG STRUGGLE FOR THEM TO ADJUST TO THE REALITY OF PASTORS' WIVES. I HAVE SEEN MANY WOMEN LIKE THAT, WHO FAILED TO GIVE THE NECESSARY SUPPORT TO THEIR HUSBANDS, CLAIMING THAT "HE IS THE ONE THAT IS CALLED, NOT ME". IGNORANCE OF WHAT IS DEMANDED OF A PASTOR'S WIFE IS SERIOUSLY LACKING IN THOSE WOMEN AND INFERIORITY COMPLEX IS ALSO A GIANT CONFRONTING THEM.

2. PASTORS HAVE NOT BEEN TOO WISE IN THEIR CHOICE OF WIVES

LOTS OF PASTORS HAVE MARRIED WRONGLY AND IT HAS HAD ADVERSE EFFECTS ON THEIR MINISTRIES. EVEN, BIG TIME PREACHERS ARE NOT LEFT OUT IN THIS MESS. MANY HAVE CHOSEN WIVES ANYHOW AND THOSE WIVES HAVE BEEN THE COG IN THE WHEEL OF PROGRESS OF THEIR MINISTRIES. JOHN

WESLEY HAD A VERY HARD TIME WITH HIS WIFE. SHE USED TO PESTER MEMBERS WITH TOMATOES AND SHE WAS A SOURCE OF HEARTACHE TO HIM THROUGHOUT HIS MINISTRY. THOUGH WOMEN LIKE THAT ALWAYS RECEIVE JUDGMENT FROM THE LORD, YET THEY WOULD HAVE DESTROYED THINGS.

3. MINISTERS' WIVES NEED TO BE ENLIGHTENED

MANY OF THE MISDEMENOURS OF PASTORS' WIVES STEM FROM THE FACT THAT THEY WERE NOT PROPERLY TAUGHT. THERE IS NO SCHOOL THAT TEACHES HOW TO BE A GOOD PASTOR'S WIFE. MANY SINCERE WOMEN WHO FOUND THEMSELVES AS MINISTERS' WIVES HAVE HAD TO LEARN THROUGH TRIAL AND ERRORS.

THE PLACE OF A MINISTER'S WIFE IS VERY CRUCIAL TO THE SUCCESS OF HER HUSBAND'S MINISTRY, THE MORE REASON I'M WRITING THIS BOOK TO THROW THE NEEDED LIGHT ON COGENT AREAS. A PASTOR WAS MALICIOUSLY TRANSFERRED FROM A GROWING CITY CHURCH TO A VERY SMALL CHURCH IN A RURAL AREA. ON THEIR FIRST DAY IN THE NEW CHURCH, ONLY THE PASTOR AND HIS WIFE WERE IN THE SERVICE. BUT THE WIFE STOOD BY HIM AND PROMISED TO FAST AND PRAY FOR THREE YEARS, IF GOD WILL SEND THE PEOPLE. BY THEIR FIRST YEAR IN THAT CHURCH THERE WERE OVERFLOWING

THE MATURED MINISTER'S WIFE

IN THIS FIRST PART OF THE BOOK, WE
SHALL BE EXAMINING THE LIFE, POWER,
POSITION, RESPONSIBILITIES AND CHARACTER
OF A GODLY PASTOR'S WIFE.
I WILL BE USING PASTOR'S WIFE MUCH
MORE OFTEN THAN MINISTER'S WIFE. BUT
I'M REALLY REFERRING TO ALL THOSE
WONDERFUL WOMEN THAT ARE MARRIED TO
GOSPEL MINISTERS, EITHER THE HUSBAND
IS LEADING A CHURCH OR NOT.

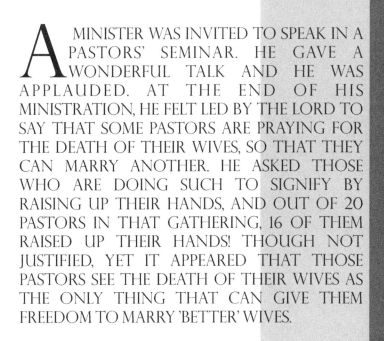

WHO IS A PASTOR'S WIFE?

CHAPTER ONE

A MINISTER WAS INVITED TO SPEAK IN A PASTORS' SEMINAR. HE GAVE A WONDERFUL TALK AND HE WAS APPLAUDED. AT THE END OF HIS MINISTRATION, HE FELT LED BY THE LORD TO SAY THAT SOME PASTORS ARE PRAYING FOR THE DEATH OF THEIR WIVES, SO THAT THEY CAN MARRY ANOTHER. HE ASKED THOSE WHO ARE DOING SUCH TO SIGNIFY BY RAISING UP THEIR HANDS, AND OUT OF 20 PASTORS IN THAT GATHERING, 16 OF THEM RAISED UP THEIR HANDS! THOUGH NOT JUSTIFIED, YET IT APPEARED THAT THOSE PASTORS SEE THE DEATH OF THEIR WIVES AS THE ONLY THING THAT CAN GIVE THEM FREEDOM TO MARRY 'BETTER' WIVES.

THE POSITIVE OR NEGATIVE INFLUENCE OF A

PASTOR'S WIFE IN TODAY'S MINISTRY CANNOT BE OVEREMPHASIZED. EVERY GODLY PASTOR IS A PRODUCT OF A GODLY WIFE AND EVERY UNGODLY AND UNSETTLED PASTOR IS THE PRODUCT OF A BAD WIFE. AND EVERY GODLY CHILD OF ANY PASTOR IS A DIRECT PRODUCT OF THE MOTHER. A PASTOR'S WIFE HAS INCREASINGLY GREAT ROLES TO PLAY IN THE LIFE AND MINISTRY OF THE HUSBAND.

> *A pastor's wife must be a woman's woman, one woman in a million.*

IT IS ALSO IMPORTANT TO ESTABLISH THIS FACT EARLY THAT NOT EVERY WOMAN CAN BE A PASTOR'S WIFE. IT IS NOT EVERY FEMALE THAT CAN FUNCTION IN THE ROLE OF A MINISTER'S WIFE. PASTORAL AND MINISTERIAL ASSIGNMENTS ARE HEAVY RESPONSIBILITIES THAT IT WILL TAKE A WOMAN OF HIGHER VIRTUES WITH GREAT CAPACITIES TO BE A GOOD WIFE TO A PASTOR. MANY WOMEN THAT MARRIED PASTORS ARE FALLING ABYSMALLY TODAY SIMPLY BECAUSE THEY LACKED THE REQUISITE VIRTUES AND CAPACITIES TO HANDLE THE HEAVY RESPONSIBILITIES OF PASTORAL MINISTRY. THE GREAT RESPONSIBILITIES OF THE MINISTRY DIRECTLY PLACE HEAVY BURDEN ON EVERY PASTOR'S WIFE.

BEING A GOOD AND GODLY PASTOR'S WIFE IS MUCH MORE THAN THE FAME, HONOUR, CLOTHINGS, SEATING POSITIONS AND GLAMOUR ASSOCIATED WITH THAT ROLE TODAY. LOTS OF WOMEN OF

TODAY ONLY SEE THE OUTWARD HAPPENINGS OF BEING PASTORS' WIVES AND KNOW NEXT TO NOTHING ABOUT THE BURDEN, SACRIFICE AND PAIN THAT PASTORS' WIVES HAVE TO ENDURE AND PUT UP WITH ON DAILY BASIS.

A TRUE PASTOR'S WIFE

"Likewise, their wives must be reverent, not slanderers, temperate, faithful in all things."

- I TIM. 3:11

"The older women likewise, that they be reverent in behaviour, not slanderers, not given to much wine, teachers of good things that they admonish the young women to love their husbands, to love their children, to be discreet, chaste, homemakers, good, obedient to their own husbands, that the word of God may not be blasphemed"

TITUS 2:3-5.

THESE TWO SCRIPTURAL PASSAGES ARE VERY CLEAR ABOUT THE DESIRABLE QUALITIES THAT A PASTOR'S WIFE MUST POSSESS. A PASTOR'S WIFE MUST BE A WOMAN'S WOMAN, ONE WOMAN IN A MILLION. A TRUE PARAGON OF SPIRITUAL BEAUTY, MEEK, GODLY AND WITH A KIND SPIRIT. SHE MUST BE A PICTURE OF GODLY REFERENCES, RESPECTFUL, GOOD BEHAVIOUR AND SERIOUS COMPORTMENT. SHE MUST BE KIND-HEARTED, WISE, LOVING, RESERVED AND LISTEN MORE WITH HER EARS THAN SPEAKING WITH HER MOUTH. SHE MUST SHOW TRUE LOVE, DEVOTION AND RESPECT TO HER HUSBAND AND BE FAITHFUL TO HIM

IN EVERY AREA. SHE MUST RAISE UP HER CHILDREN IN THE FEAR AND WAYS OF THE LORD. SHE MUST NOT BE IDLE OR BE A BUSY BODY IN CHURCH MATTERS.

SHE MUST KEEP HERSELF PURE, NEAT, GODLY AND SINCERE. A TRUE SPIRITUAL GIANT IN PRAYERS AND INTERCESSION FOR THE HUSBAND AND MINISTRY. SHE MUST BE A GOOD HOME MAKER AND TURN THE HOME INTO A PLACE OF REST AND SECURITY FROM THE STORMS OF LIFE. SHE MUST BE A TRUE BIBLICAL WIFE, NOT A CULTURAL OR MODERN DAY WIFE. A TRUE WIFE, NOT A KNIFE, A PILLAR NOT A CATERPILLAR, A MAKER AT HOME, NOT A DESTROYER. A MATURED, GROWING AND SPIRITUALLY DEEP WOMAN OF FAITH AND PRAYER, NOT A TALKATIVE, QUARRELSOME, DEMONIC AND ANTAGONISTIC WOMAN. A TRUE BLESSING, NOT A CURSE TO THE HUSBAND. A BLISS, NOT A HISS.

"Wives, likewise, be submissive to your own husbands… for in this manner, in former times, the holy women who trusted in God also adorned themselves, being submissive to their own husbands, as Sarah obeyed Abraham, calling him lord, whose daughters you are if you do good and are not afraid with any terror."

- I PET. 3:1,5,6

As a woman, you are either the daughter of Sarah or daughter of Eve by your characters and lifestyles.

18

HOW MANY PASTORS' WIVES CAN CLAIM TO MEASURE UP TO THIS SCRIPTURAL QUALITIES TODAY? I KNOW THIS IS A VERY TALL ORDER FOR VERY MANY OF YOU. BUT YOU HAVE NO CHOICE, THESE ARE THE QUALITIES THAT YOU MUST IMBIBE IN YOUR LIFE AS A WOMAN. IF YOU WANT TO BE A GOOD AND GODLY MINISTER'S WIFE THAT GOD WILL BLESS CONTINUALLY, YOU MUST PRAY AND WORK THESE QUALITIES INTO YOUR LIFE AND CONDUCT. IF YOU DON'T WANT TO BE A WIFE WHOSE HUSBAND WILL BE PRAYING FOR HER PREMATURE DEATH, THEN YOU MUST MEASURE UP TO THIS BIBLICAL QUALITIES OF A PASTOR'S WIFE.

TODAY, DIVORCE AND SEPARATION HAS GRADUALLY CREPT INTO THE CHURCH AND IT'S A GROWING PLAGUE, SIMPLY BECAUSE PASTORS' WIVES ARE NOT DISPLAYING THESE QUALITIES IN THEIR LIVES AND

DAUGHTER OF EVE	DAUGHTER OF SARAH
1. SHE IS ONLY NOBLE BY BIRTH.	1. SHE BECOMES NOBLE BY COVENANT AND CHARACTER.
2. HER NOBILITY IS CARNAL AND SECULAR.	2. HER NOBILITY IS SPIRITUAL AND GODLY.
3. BAD EXAMPLE OF A WIFE.	3. GOOD EXAMPLE OF A GODLY WIFE.
4. HAS NEGATIVE INFLUENCE ON HER HUSBAND.	4. HAS POSITIVE INFLUENCE ON HER HUSBAND.
5. AFFECTS HER OFFSPRINGS AND THE WORLD NEGATIVELY.	5. HAS POSITIVE INFLUENCE ON HER CHILDREN AND THE WORLD.

19

6. SHE PIONEERS STUBBORN AND DISOBEDIENT LIFESTYLE FOR WOMEN.	6. SHE PIONEERS SUBMISSION, HUMILITY AND OBEDIENT LIVING FOR WIVES.
7. SHE CALLS HER HUSBAND SLAVE.	7. SHE CALLS HER HUSBAND LORD.
8. SHE IS THE LEADER OF REBELLIOUS WOMEN THAT COMPETE WITH THEIR HUSBANDS.	8. SHE IS THE LEADER OF SUBMISSIVE WIVES THAT COMPLEMENT THEIR HUSBANDS.
9. SHE LISTENS TO SATANIC SERMONS AND YIELDS TO DECEPTION.	9. SHE LISTENS TO GOD AND HER HUSBAND AND OBEYS HIM.
10. MOTHER OF SORROW. SHE BROUGHT SORROW TO ISAAC AND HELPS HER HUSBAND TO LOSE HIS ESTATE.	10. MOTHER OF LAUGHTER. SHE BROUGHT JOY TO THE WORLD.
11. SHE IS EARTHLY AND WORLDLY MINDED.	11. SHE IS SPIRITUAL AND HEAVENLY MINDED.
12. SHE BROUGHT THE ANGER OF GOD UPON HERSELF AND HER GENERATION.	12. SHE OBTAINED THE FAVOUR OF GOD FOR HERSELF AND GENERATIONS YET UNBORN.
13. MOTHER OF ALL DEMONIZED WOMEN. JEZEBEL OF OUR TIME.	13. MOTHER OF ALL SPIRIT-FILLED WOMEN WHO ARE GODLY TODAY.

FAILING TO TEACH THE CHRISTIAN WOMEN TOO. LOTS OF PASTORS ARE DIVORCING THEIR WIVES BECAUSE THEIR WIVES HAVE FAILED TO IMBIBE THE

QUALITIES OF GODLY PASTORS' WIVES. TO STEM THE TIDE, MINISTERS' WIVES MUST GO BACK TO BEING BIBLICAL WIVES AND START TEACHING OTHER CHRISTIAN WOMEN TOO, BOTH BY PRACTICE AND PRECEPT.

DAUGHTER OF SARAH OR DAUGHTER OF EVE

IN THE SCRIPTURE QUOTED ABOVE, THE BIBLE CALLS WOMEN WHO OBEYED THEIR HUSBANDS AS DAUGHTERS OF SARAH. WOMEN WHO ARE SUBMISSIVE AND GODLY WIVES TO THEIR HUSBANDS ARE OFFSPRINGS OF SARAH, THE GREAT WIFE OF ABRAHAM, THE FRIEND OF GOD. LIKEWISE, WOMEN WHO CAUSED REBELLION CAN BE REFERRED TO AS DAUGHTERS OF EVE, BECAUSE THOSE ARE THE TWO GREAT WOMEN IN THE BIBLE THAT EVERY OTHER WOMEN ORIGINATED FROM. SO AS A WOMAN, YOU ARE EITHER THE DAUGHTER OF SARAH OR DAUGHTER OF EVE BY YOUR CHARACTERS AND LIFESTYLES.

TO HAVE A COMPREHENSIVE UNDERSTANDING OF THESE TWO WOMEN, ALLOW ME TO DO A GOOD COMPARISON, USING THE ATTRIBUTES THAT WERE FEASIBLE IN THE LIVES OF THESE TWO WOMEN:-

AS YOU CAN SEE, MANY PASTORS' WIVES POSSESSED MORE OF THE ATTRIBUTES OF THE DAUGHTER OF EVE THAN THAT OF SARAH TODAY. THERE ARE MANY DAUGHTERS OF EVE IN THE PARSONAGE TODAY. THEY DISPLAY UNGODLY CHARACTERS OF DECEPTION, REBELLION AND GENERAL LACK OF FEAR OF THE

LORD IN ALL THEY DO. IN THE SCRIPTURE, YOU HAVE WOMEN SUCH AS REBECCA, DELILAH, JEZEBEL, VASHTI, MICAH AND SAPHIRA WHO ALL DISPLAYED THE CHARACTERISTICS OF THE DAUGHTERS OF EVE, AND WERE JUDGED BY THEIR BAD MANNERS AND GOD.

LIKEWISE, THERE ARE STORIES OF PASTORS' WIVES TODAY WHO STEAL CHURCH FUNDS, SLEEP AROUND WITH MEN, FIGHT CHURCH MEMBERS AND STRUGGLE THE PULPIT WITH THEIR HUSBANDS, EVEN WHEN THEY DON'T HAVE THE SKILL TO COMMUNICATE WITH PEOPLE. IT ONLY GOES TO SHOW THAT THEY ARE DAUGHTERS OF EVE AND NOT THAT OF GODLY SARAH.

THE MAKING OF A GOOD PASTOR'S WIFE

EVERY WOMAN WAS ORIGINALLY A DAUGHTER OF

THE MATURED PASTOR'S WIFE

I KNOW A PASTOR THAT WAS VERY VERSATILE. HE ONCE SERVED AS THE PRINCIPAL OF HIS CHURCH'S BIBLE SCHOOL. HE SERVED THE CHURCH FOR MANY YEARS MERITORIOUSLY UNTIL THE LORD CALLED HIM TO GO OUT AND START HIS OWN MINISTRY. HE OBEYED AND IN THE SPACE OF SEVEN YEARS HAVE 14 BRANCHES. BUT THE WIFE REFUSED TO FOLLOW HIM. SHE REMAINED WITH THE FORMER CHURCH AND DID EVERYTHING TO FRUSTRATE THE NEW MINISTRY OF THE HUSBAND. SHE WANTED HIM BACK IN THEIR FORMER CHURCH. WELL, AFTER SOME FEW YEARS, THE HUSBAND ACCEDED TO THE INSISTENCE OF THE WIFE AND PACKED UP HIS THRIVING MINISTRY, CLOSED DOWN THE BRANCHES AND CAME BACK TO THE FORMER CHURCH. NOT QUITE TWO YEARS AFTER, HE BECAME PARALYZED

AND DIED LATER. THE IMMATURITY OF THE WIFE CONTRIBUTED MAJORLY TO THE DEATH OF THE HUSBAND AND HIS BLOSSOMING MINISTRY.

SO MANY WOMEN HAVE BECOME PASTORS' WIVES WITHOUT ADEQUATE PREPARATION FOR IT. MANY HAVE NO TRAINING FOR THE HEAVY RESPONSIBILITIES OF

> *Sarah was a picture of a matured Pastor's wife. She was holy, humble, spiritual, submissive and exemplary.*

BEING MINISTERS' WIVES. MAJORITY MARRIED THEIR HUSBAND WHEN THEY WERE NOT CHRISTIANS, OR WERE ORDINARY CHRISTIANS WITHOUT HAVING THE THOUGHT THAT THEY WOULD EVENTUALLY BECOME PASTORS' WIVES. AND MANY OF SUCH WOMEN ARE ILL-PREPARED FOR THE HIGH EXPECTATIONS AND DEMAND OF PASTORS' WIVES IN TODAY'S SOCIETY. IMMATURE BEHAVIOURS, CARNAL ATTITUDES AND DISAPPROVING VALUES WHICH HAS BROUGHT DISREPUTE AND DISDAIN TO THE PARSONAGE ARE THE OUTCOME.

EVERY PASTOR'S WIFE MUST SEEK TO BECOME A TRULY MATURED PERSON. AND IT TAKES MUCH DEVELOPMENT, SACRIFICE AND DETERMINATION TO BECOME A MATURED PASTOR'S WIFE. AND IT IS WHEN YOU BECOME ONE THAT YOU CAN TRULY ENJOY GOD, YOUR MARRIAGE AND YOUR LIFE.

BIBLICAL FOUNDATION

24

"Likewise, ye wives, be in subjection to your own husbands; that, if any obey not the word, they also may without the word be won by the conversation of the wives; While they behold your chaste conversation coupled with fear. Whose adorning let it not be that outward adorning of plaiting the hair, and of wearing of gold, or of putting on of apparel; But let it be the hidden man of the heart, in that which is not corruptible, even the ornament of a meek and quiet spirit, which is in the sight of God of great price. For after this manner in the old time the holy women also, who trusted in God, adorned themselves, being in subjection unto their own husbands: Even as Sara obeyed Abraham, calling him lord: whose daughters ye are, as long as ye do well, and are not afraid with any amazement."

‑ I PET. 3:1‑6

"And let these also first be proved; then let them use the office of a deacon, being found blameless. Even so must their wives be grave, not slanderers, sober, faithful in all things. Let the deacons be the husbands of one wife, ruling their children and their own houses well."

‑ I TIM. 3:10‑12

SARAH WAS A PICTURE OF A MATURED PASTOR'S WIFE. SHE WAS HOLY, HUMBLE, SPIRITUAL, SUBMISSIVE AND EXEMPLARY. SHE WAS A LESSON TO OTHER WOMEN ON HOW TO LIVE. SHE LIVED A CREDIBLE AND INSPIRING LIFE. SHE BECAME THE MOTHER OF ALL GODLY WIVES AND GREAT MOTHERS. SHE DISPLAYED MUCH MATURITY IN HER RELATIONSHIP WITH HER

HUSBAND AND GOD. EVERY PASTOR'S WIFE MUST TRULY BECOME THE DAUGHTER OF SARAH IN THIS REGARD.

THE MATURITY OF THE PASTOR'S WIFE HAS MUCH TO DO WITH HER LIFE. YOU CANNOT BEHAVE HIGHER THAN YOUR MATURITY LEVEL. YOUR PEACE AND JOY WILL BE DETERMINED BY YOUR MATURITY. IF YOU ARE IMMATURE, YOU WILL BRING LOTS OF HEARTACHE TO YOURSELF. YOUR RESPECT AND RESULT WILL BE LACKING WHEN YOU BEHAVE IMMATURELY. WITHOUT DEEP AND CONTINUOUS MATURITY, YOU WILL BRING LOTS OF RUIN TO YOURSELF, YOUR HUSBAND AND YOUR CHILDREN.

TAKE NOTE OF THESE BIBLE WOMEN:-
A.   ELIZABETH BEHAVED MATUREDLY INSPITE OF HER YEARS OF BARRENNESS (LUKE 1:5-7).
B.   ABIGAIL WAS A PICTURE OF MATURITY IN STOPPING CERTAIN DESTRUCTION OF HER FAMILY (I SAM. 25:10-31).
C.   THE SYCOPHENICIAN WOMAN BEHAVED MATUREDLY INSPITE OF ABUSE TO RESCUE HER DAUGHTER (MATT. 15:22-28).

AS A FORMAL DEFINITION, MATURITY IS THE ABILITY TO DO WHAT IS RIGHT, IRRESPECTIVE OF HOW YOU FEEL; IT IS SEEING THINGS FROM BALANCED ANGLES, THE GRACE TO ALWAYS ACT RIGHTLY AND NOT REACTING TO SITUATIONS; FREEDOM FROM FRETTING, WHINING AND JEALOUSY. IT IS A LARGE HEART TO ACCOMMODATE, OVERLOOK INSULTS, FORGIVE AND FORBEAR WITH OTHERS; GETTING OVER YOUR HURTS AND A BROAD SHOULDER TO CARRY BURDENS WITHOUT BREAKING DOWN.

MATURITY DOESN'T ANSWER TO AGE, EXPERIENCE, CLASS OR STATUS. IT ANSWERS TO EXPERIENCES, PERSONAL DEVELOPMENT AND GROWTH. YOUR MATURITY WILL BE GREATLY ENHANCED BY YOUR DEEP RELATIONSHIP WITH GOD IN PRAYERS, HIS WORD AND EXPOSURES. PERSONAL ENCOUNTERS WITH THE LORD AND GODLY MENTORING WILL ALSO HELP YOUR MATURITY IN NO SMALL MEASURE.

GOD SOMETIMES USE SUFFERINGS AND PAINS TO DEVELOP OUR SPIRITUAL STRENGTH AND GODLY CHARACTER THAT WILL HELP US TO HANDLE THINGS IN ADMIRABLE WAYS. EVERY PASTOR'S WIFE MUST DEVELOP SPIRITUAL, MENTAL, RELATIONAL, MINISTERIAL, FAMILY AND PERSONAL MATURITY. IT IS VERY CRUCIAL TO THE SUCCESS OF YOUR LIFE. YOUR ALL ROUND MATURITY IS FUNDAMENTAL TO THE SUCCESS OF YOUR LIFE AND HOME.

> *Every Pastor's wife must develop spiritual, mental, relational, ministerial, family and personal maturity.*

PRESSURES ON PASTORS' WIVES

YES, PASTORS' WIVES FACE LOTS OF PRESSURES TODAY. JUST AS THE ROLE OF PASTORS AND GOSPEL MINISTERS ARE BEING INCREASINGLY SCRUTINIZED BY THE SOCIETY, SO ALSO THE PRESSURES ARE MOUNTING ON PASTORS' WIVES. THE PEOPLE'S

27

EXPECTATIONS OF THE MINISTER'S WIFE IS VERY HIGH. SHE IS EXPECTED TO BE UP AND DOING, TO BE A GOOD WIFE, GODLY MOTHER, DYNAMIC MINISTER AND A CAPABLE REPLACEMENT OF HER HUSBAND.

FURTHERMORE, FINANCIAL PRESSURES COME BECAUSE LOTS OF PASTORS ARE POORLY RENUMERATED, AND 80% OF THEIR WIVES ARE CAREER WOMEN. LOTS OF PASTORS' WIVES WORK OUTSIDE THE CHURCH AS BANKERS, TEACHERS, BUSINESS WOMEN AND PROFESSIONALS, IN ORDER TO MAKE ENDS MEET AT THE HOME FRONT. AND THEIR ABSENCE FROM HOME AND MINISTRY ALWAYS HAVE NEGATIVE CONSEQUENCES ON THE HUSBAND AND WORK.

FOR ONE, WOMEN PREDATORS TAKE ADVANTAGE OF THE WIFE'S ABSENCE TO TEMPT THE PASTOR INTO SIN THROUGH SEDUCTIVE WORDS DURING DECEITFUL COUNSELING SESSIONS. PASTORS' WIVES ALSO FACE SPIRITUAL ATTACKS AND PRESSURES TO COMPROMISE SO THAT THE HUSBAND CAN BE INCAPACITATED SPIRITUALLY. THERE ARE LOTS OF MEMBERS THAT WANT THE PASTOR'S WIFE DEAD, SO THAT THEY CAN MARRY THE PASTOR.

I HAVE HANDLED CASES OF MEMBERS USING DEMONIC POWERS TO AFFLICT THE PASTOR'S WIFE WITH SICKNESS SO AS TO KILL HER IN ORDER FOR THEM TO MARRY THE PASTOR AND RUIN HIS MINISTRY. SOME WOMEN IN A PARTICULAR CHURCH GATHERED TOGETHER TO PRAY FOR THE DEATH OF THE PASTOR'S WIFE BECAUSE SHE IS A STRONG PILLAR OF SUPPORT BEHIND HIM. UNFORTUNATELY, LOTS OF

PASTORS' WIVES ARE IGNORANT OF THESE SPIRITUAL CROSS-CURRENTS AND ARE PRAYERLESS, THE MORE REASON SOME OF THEM ARE DYING MYSTERIOUSLY.

THE WIFE OF GOSPEL MINISTERS ARE ENDANGERED SPECIES SIMPLY BECAUSE THEY ARE LARGELY UNTRAINED AND UNEQUIPPED FOR THE PRESSURES THAT DAILY COME UPON THEM. FINANCIAL, MATERIAL, MINISTERIAL, SOCIETAL, MENTAL AND SPIRITUAL PRESSURES ARE DAILY MAKING THE PARSONAGE MUCH MORE DIFFICULT THAN EVER BEFORE. HOWEVER, WOMEN IN BIBLE TIMES SOAKED UP THESE PRESSURES AS A RESULT OF THEIR SPIRITUAL MATURITY AND I BELIEVE THAT WIVES OF MINISTERS OF TODAY SHOULD BE ABLE TO HANDLE THESE CHALLENGES, PROVIDED THEY IMPROVE THEIR MATURITY LEVEL.

IMMATURITY OF PASTORS' WIVES

IMMATURITY IS ADDICTION TO CHILDISH BEHAVIOURS, AND LOTS OF PASTORS' WIVES TODAY ARE DISPLAYING CRASS IGNORANCE AND IMMATURITY IN HANDLING THE CHALLENGES OF MINISTRY AND THE PARSONAGE HERE AND THERE.

A CERTAIN PASTOR'S WIFE SPONSORED THE CHURCH OF THE HUSBAND FINANCIALLY. THE NEXT THING IS THAT SHE STARTED TO DOMINATE THE AFFAIRS OF THE CHURCH AND WANTED TO BE ORDAINED AS A PASTOR, EVEN THOUGH GOD HAS NOT CALLED HER INTO ANY OF THE FIVE-FOLD MINISTRY ROLES. I HAVE HEARD OF MANY PASTORS' WIVES WHO REFUSED TO ATTEND THE CHURCH OF THE HUSBAND BECAUSE

ONE FLIMSY EXCUSE OR THE OTHER. THIS IS A CHILDISH ATTITUDE!

WHEN YOU GO ROUND TO REPORT YOUR HUSBAND TO CHURCH MEMBERS AND COMMITTEE PEOPLE, YOU ARE DISPLAYING HIGH LEVEL OF IMMATURITY. NAGGING, COMPLAINING, SUSPECTING YOUR HUSBAND AND THEREBY STAYING AROUND DURING HIS COUNSELING SESSIONS SO THAT NO WOMAN WILL SNATCH HIM FROM YOU IS ANOTHER SIGN OF IMMATURE ATTITUDES. GOING ROUND TO BORROW CLOTHINGS, FOOD STUFFS AND MONEY FROM MEMBERS; COMING LATE TO CHURCH AND SETTING BAD EXAMPLES FOR OTHERS SHOW THAT YOUR MATURITY LEVEL IS STILL VERY LOW.

WHEN YOU TAKE YOUR CAREER AS MUCH MORE IMPORTANT THAN SUPPORTING HIM AND THE MINISTRY, THEN YOU NEED SOME GROWING UP TO DO. WHEN YOU DO NOTHING TO DEVELOP YOURSELF SPIRITUALLY AND MINISTERIALLY, THEREBY FINDING IT DIFFICULT TO LEAD PRAYER EFFECTIVELY, READ THE SCRIPTURE LIVELY AND CONTRIBUTE MEANINGFULLY IN THE CHURCH, IT SIMPLY SHOWS THAT YOU ARE STILL IMMATURE. WHEN YOU FIGHT AND QUARREL WITH CHURCH MEMBERS, SIMPLY BECAUSE THEY DON'T GIVE YOU THE RESPECT YOU FEEL YOU DESERVE AND YOU ARE MAKING THINGS DIFFICULT AT HOME FOR HIM AS A RESULT OF THAT, THEN YOU ARE YET TO MATURE WELL.

WHEN YOU DIVULGE INFORMATION TO MEMBERS WITHOUT YOUR HUSBAND'S CONSENT; WHEN YOU FAIL TO KEEP THE HOME RUNNING IN HIS ABSENCE;

WHEN YOU ARE THE CHIEF ANTAGONIST OF HIS MINISTRY, COMPLAINING, FAULT-FINDING, AND MURMURING, THEN YOU ARE SHOWING THAT YOU ARE STILL CHILDISH IN YOUR ATTITUDE AND BEHAVIOURS. WHEN YOU LISTEN TO UNGODLY COUNSELS AND YOU BECOME STUBBORN, ARROGANT AND DISOBEDIENT TO HIM, IT GOES TO SHOW THAT YOU ARE YET TO GROW UP TO WHERE GOD WILL REALLY BLESS YOU. BROKEN LIVES, BROKEN BONES, BROKEN HEARTS, BROKEN MARRIAGES AND BROKEN FUTURES ARE THE ADVERSE EFFECTS OF IMMATURITY ON THE PART OF PASTORS' WIVES.

QUALITIES OF A MATURED PASTOR'S WIFE

IT WILL TAKE SERIOUS AND CONCERTED EFFORTS ON YOUR PART TO BECOME A MATURED WIFE TO YOUR HUSBAND. BECOMING A MATURED WOMAN AND WIFE DEMANDS THAT YOU INCULCATE THESE QUALITIES INTO YOUR DAILY LIVING:-

Until your level of understanding changes, you will continue to be childish in your behaviours.

1. PROPER UNDERSTANDING

"...and the Lord give thee understanding in all things."

- II TIM. 2:7

UNDERSTANDING IS VERY CRUCIAL TO YOUR

31

MATURITY. RATHER THAN SEEKING TO BE UNDERSTOOD, TRY TO UNDERSTAND YOURSELF, YOUR ROLE, YOUR HUSBAND AND THE CALL OF GOD UPON HIS LIFE. WITHOUT GOOD UNDERSTANDING, YOU CANNOT FUNCTION MATUREDLY. UNTIL YOUR LEVEL OF UNDERSTANDING CHANGES, YOU WILL CONTINUE TO BE CHILDISH IN YOUR BEHAVIOURS. GOOD UNDERSTANDING IS THE FIRST STEP IN ATTAINING GREAT MATURITY LEVEL.

2.   WISDOM

DIVINE WISDOM TO RELATE WITH ALL AND SUNDRY IS GREATLY NEEDED. WISDOM IS THE RIGHT APPLICATION OF KNOWLEDGE. YOU MUST BE WISE IN YOUR WAYS AND DEALINGS WITH CHURCH MEMBERS AND PEOPLE IN THE MINISTRY. FOOLS SUFFER WHERE THE WISE PROSPER. ABIGAIL WAS A WOMAN OF WISDOM. SHE WAS FULL OF TACT AND TOOK PROACTIVE STEPS TO SAVE HER FAMILY. EVERY PASTOR'S WIFE MUST DISPLAY WISDOM IN RELATIONSHIP WITH OTHERS, WITHIN AND OUTSIDE THE MINISTRY.

> *"She openeth her mouth with wisdom; and in her tongue is the law of kindness."*
>
> - PROV. 31:26

3.   HUMILITY

> *"Though the LORD be high, yet hath he respect unto the lowly; but the proud he knoweth afar off."*
>
> - PSALM 138:6

IT IS ONLY THE LOWLY IN HEART AND LIFE THAT GOD WILL RESPECT. HE STAYS FAR AWAY FROM THE PROUD AND COCKY. MATURED WOMEN ARE HUMBLE WOMEN, LIKE SARAH, WHO HUMBLED HERSELF AND CALLED HER HUSBAND LORD. SHE ALSO OBEYED HIM IN TOTALITY. WOMEN THAT REBEL, DISOBEY AND DISPLEASE THEIR HUSBANDS, SIMPLY BECAUSE THEY ARE PASTORS ARE SURELY PROUD AND THE LORD IS FAR AWAY FROM THEM. SUBMISSION AND RESPECT TO YOUR HUSBAND, INSPITE OF YOUR STATUS AND HIS INADEQUACIES ARE SIGNS OF HUMILITY THAT GOD HONOURS.

4. PRAYERFULNESS

ELIZABETH WAS A WOMAN OF PRAYER AND FAITH. SHE SUPPORTED HER HUSBAND'S MINISTRY WITH HER PRAYERS, INSPITE OF THEIR SEEMING BARRENNESS. SHE WAS PRAYERFUL AND TOOK EVERYTHING TO GOD IN PRAYER. A MATURED PASTOR'S WIFE MUST BE A PRAYER GIANT. RATHER THAN BE COMPLAINING, CRITICAL AND NAGGING THE HUSBAND, SHE TAKES EVERYTHING TO GOD IN EARNEST PRAYERS. SHE INTERCEDES FOR HER HUSBAND AND CHILDREN CONSTANTLY. THROUGH HER PRAYERS, SHE DRAWS DOWN THE POWER OF GOD INTO HER HOME. SHE BELIEVES STRONGLY AND PRACTICE THIS SCRIPTURE ALWAYS:

> *"Be careful for nothing, but in everything by prayer and supplication with thanksgiving, let your requests be made known unto God."*
> - PHIL. 4:6

5. SPIRIT-FILLED

ELIZABETH WAS HOLY SPIRIT POSSESSED. SHE WALKED IN THE SPIRIT AND WAS A PROPHETESS OF HER HOME. SHE WAS FILLED WITH GOD'S SPIRIT AND WAS SPIRITUALLY SENSITIVE TO THE VOICE OF GOD. SHE HAD NO ROOM IN HER HEART AND LIFE FOR STRANGE SPIRITS. EVERY PASTOR'S WIFE MUST BE FILLED WITH THE HOLY SPIRIT OF GOD, WITH ATTENDANT FRUITS OF PEACE, LOVE, JOY, GOODNESS AND KINDNESS MANIFESTING IN HER DAILY LIFE.

THERE MUST BE NO ROOM FOR DEMONIC AND OCCULTIC SPIRITS IN YOUR LIFE. YOU MUST HAVE NO ROOM FOR CARNAL AND EVIL SPIRITS TO RULE IN YOUR HEART. YOU MUST RATHER BE FILLED WITH THE GOOD AND HOLY SPIRIT OF GOD. FOR THE SPIRIT YOU ARE FILLED WITH WILL SURELY AFFECT YOU, YOUR MANNERS, YOUR HUSBAND AND CHILDREN. UNFORTUNATELY, MANY SO-CALLED PASTORS' WIVES ARE FILLED WITH STRANGE AND EVIL SPIRITS, THAT IS WHY THEY MANIFEST THE CHARACTERISTICS OF THE DAUGHTERS OF EVE IN THEIR DAILY LIVING. WHAT A SHAME!

6. INNER BEAUTY

IT WAS SAID OF SARAH THAT SHE HAD "THE ORNAMENT OF A MEEK AND QUIET SPIRIT, WHICH IN THE SIGHT OF GOD IS OF GREAT PRICE" (I PET. 3:4).

THE TRUE BEAUTY OF A PASTOR'S WIFE MUST BE AN INNER ONE; MEEK, QUIET, NOBLE, GODLY AND SINCERE HEART. TROUBLESOME, BRAWLING AND CANTERKEROUS SPIRIT ARE UNBECOMING OF A

YOUR IMPACT IN THE MINISTRY OF YOUR HUSBAND

A PASTOR FRIEND OF MINE MARRIED A LADY THAT WAS A THORN IN HIS LIFE. SHE HAD THE HABIT OF CONSTANTLY OPPRESSING HIM, AND ONE DAY, HE SNAPPED AND THEY HAD A FIGHT. I WAS CALLED TO SETTLE THE QUARREL AND THE WIFE TOLD ME POINTEDLY THAT I SHOULD NOT BOTHER MYSELF BECAUSE SHE IS GOING TO SCATTER THE CHURCH THE FOLLOWING SUNDAY. I TRIED IN VAIN TO PLACATE HER BUT SHE WOULD NOT BUDGE. ON SUNDAY, SHE WOKE UP EARLY AND WENT TO CHURCH. SHE WORE A MINI-SKIRT WITH SPAGHETTI BLOUSE AND SAT ON THE ALTAR. SHE OPENED HER LAPS, REVEALING HER PRIVATE PART, BEHOLD, SHE WORE NO PANT! MEMBERS RAN AWAY AND THE CHURCH HAD TO CLOSE DOWN AFTER FUTILE EFFORTS BY THE PASTOR. WHAT A TRAGEDY!

OVER THE YEARS, WE HAVE SEEN AGAIN AND AGAIN, THE INCREDIBLE DAMAGES THAT CAN BE DONE TO A PASTOR'S MINISTRY BY THE WIFE. A CERTAIN PASTOR'S WIFE ANNOUNCED IN THE CHURCH THAT NONE OF THE MEMBERS SHOULD VISIT THE HUSBAND FOR COUNSELING, AND IF ANYONE DOES, SHE WILL DEAL RUTHLESSLY WITH HIM/HER. WELL, THAT WAS HOW THE CHURCH LOST MAJORITY OF THE MEMBERS. THE WIFE OF A PASTOR CAN DO AND UNDO THE MINISTRY OF HER HUSBAND. LAWYERS, DOCTORS, ARCHITECTS AND GOVERNMENT OFFICIALS CAN SUCCEED IN THEIR VOCATIONS WITH LITTLE OR NO IMPACT FROM THEIR WIVES, BUT NOT SO FOR A PASTOR OR GOSPEL MINISTER. THE WIVES OF MINISTERS ARE THE MAJOR KEYS TO THE PROGRESS OR RETARDATION OF THEIR HUSBANDS' MINISTRY.

RESPONSIBILITY OF PASTORS' WIVES

SCRITURALLY, A PASTOR MUST MARRY AND HAVE A GOOD WIFE, EXCEPT THOSE WHO ARE EUNUCHS. BEING IN MINISTRY IS AN AWESOME TASK AND IT THEREFORE PLACES GREAT RESPONSIBILITIES AND EXPECTATIONS ON THE WIFE OF THE PASTOR. AS A PASTOR'S WIFE, YOU ARE THERE TO HELP HIM SUCCEED IN HIS LIFE AND CALLING

"She will do him good and not evil all the days of her life."

- PROV. 31:12

BEING A PASTOR'S WIFE DOESN'T MEAN YOU ARE AUTOMATICALLY AN ASSISTANT GENERAL OVERSEER, PASTOR, PREACHER AND LEADER IN THE CHURCH. YOU ARE FIRST AND FOREMOST A WIFE TO YOUR HUSBAND AND THAT IS WHERE YOU SHOULD STAY. YOU ARE NOT TO LORD YOUR POSITION OVER THE PEOPLE IN THE CHURCH AND THROW YOUR WEIGHT AROUND. YOU ARE NOT TO USE YOUR POSITION AS THE WIFE OF THE PASTOR TO SUBJUGATE, DOMINATE AND RULE OVER THE PEOPLE OF THE CHURCH.

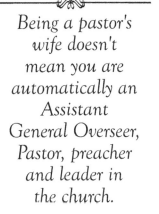

Being a pastor's wife doesn't mean you are automatically an Assistant General Overseer, Pastor, preacher and leader in the church.

A PASTOR'S WIFE USED HER ROLE TO TAKE OVER THE FINANCIAL PURSE OF THE CHURCH. SHE BECAME THE SIGNATORY TO THE ACCOUNT OF THE CHURCH AND DETERMINES HOW THE MONEY SHOULD BE SPENT. ANOTHER ONE DEFRAUDED THE CHURCH TO THE TUNE OF SEVERAL MILLIONS WHEN SHE WAS TO SUPPLY MATERIAL FOR THE HOLY COMMUNION IN THE CHURCH. WHEN THE HUGE AMOUNT SHE PRESENTED WAS QUERIED BY THE ACCOUNTANT, SHE RETORTED; 'SIGN THE MONEY OR LOSE YOUR JOB. IT IS NOT YOUR FATHER'S MONEY, BUT THAT OF THE CHURCH FOUNDED BY MY HUSBAND'. WELL, THAT IS AN UNGODLY WAY TO BE A PASTOR'S WIFE. BY HER ACTION, SHE HAS BROUGHT LARGE SCALE STEALING AND FRAUDULENT PRACTICES TO THAT CHURCH.

A TRUE PASTOR'S WIFE MUST GROW AND DEVELOP INTO MINISTERIAL POSITION IN THE CHURCH, AFTER SHE HAS TAKEN ADEQUATE CARE OF HER RESPONSIBILITIES. THE BASIC AND PRIMARY RESPONSIBILITIES OF THE WIFE OF A PASTOR IS ENCAPSULATED IN THE FOLLOWING:-

I.   **PRAYER SUPPORT** : PRAY AND LIFT HIM UP IN INTERCESSION.

II.   **PROTECTION:** BE A COVER FOR HIS INTEGRITY AND CREDIBILITY.

III.   **PROVISION:** FOOD, CARE AND NEEDS AS AT WHEN DUE.

IV.   **PARTNERSHIP:** DEVELOP YOUR PRIVATE AND PUBLIC MINISTRY AS GOD ALLOWS.

V.   **PRESERVATION:** GIVE HIM PEACE AND JOY THAT WILL KEEP HIM IN THE LORD.

YOUR PRIMARY RESPONSIBILITY IS TO YOUR HUSBAND. YOU ARE TO BE A GOOD AND GREAT WIFE TO HIM AND A LOVING MOTHER TO YOUR CHILDREN. YOUR NUMBER ONE MINISTRY IS TO MINISTER TO YOUR HUSBAND AND YOUR NUMBER TWO MINISTRY IS TO RAISE YOUR CHILDREN IN THE WAY OF THE LORD. IT IS WHEN YOU SUCCEED IN THESE TWO MINISTRIES THAT YOU CAN BE A SUCCESS IN YOUR PUBLIC OR PRIVATE MINISTRY AS THE LORD WILL GIVE THEM TO YOU.

NEGATIVE OR POSITIVE IMPACT

IT IS AN UNWRITTEN RULE THAT WIVES DO INFLUENCE THEIR HUSBANDS. THIS INFLUENCE CAN

BE NEGATIVE OR POSITIVE. TAKE THE EXAMPLE OF KING AHAB AS A CASE IN POINT;

"But there was none like unto Ahab, which did sell himself to work wickedness in the sight of the LORD, whom Jezebel his wife stirred up"
- I KINGS 21:25

HE BECAME A VERY WICKED KING AS A RESULT OF THE NEGATIVE INFLUENCE OF THE WIFE, JEZEBEL. WIVES DO INFLUENCE THEIR HUSBANDS THROUGH WORDS, ACTIONS AND CONSTANT PRESSURE. WHILE SOME MEN TRY TO RESIST, YET THE TRUTH IS THAT MOST MEN SOMEHOW SUCCUMB TO THE INFLUENCE OF THEIR WIVES SOONER OR LATER. INFLUENCING YOUR HUSBAND NEGATIVELY WILL HAVE ADVERSE EFFECT ON HIS LIFE, MINISTRY AND UPON YOU. JEZEBEL DID NOT DIE WELL DUE TO HER NEGATIVE INFLUENCE. INFLUENCING YOUR HUSBAND TO TAKE WRONG DECISIONS; SACK THOSE WHO YOU FELT ARE DISRESPECTING YOU; FIGHTING TO BE PLACED ON THE ALTAR AND DOMINATING EVERYBODY IN THE CHURCH; WILL ALL LEAD TO DOWNWARD SPIRAL OF THE CHURCH. DOMINATING AND RULING YOUR HUSBAND AT HOME WILL ERODE HIS RESPECT IN THE CHURCH AND MAKE GODLY PEOPLE TO LEAVE

> *Dominating and ruling your husband at home will erode his respect in the church and make godly people to leave enmass.*

ENMASS.

A HIGHLY ANOINTED PASTOR MARRIED A WIFE WHO USED TO BEAT HIM. ONE DAY SHE DID NOT ALLOW HIM TO COME AND CONDUCT THE WEDDING CEREMONY SLATED FOR THAT DAY IN THE CHURCH. WHEN THE CHURCH COMMITTEE WAITED AND WAITED AND THE PASTOR FAILED TO SHOW UP, THEY DECIDED TO CHECK HIM UP IN THE HOUSE. THERE THEY MET HIM ON HIS KNEES BEGGING THE WIFE, WHILE SHE WAS TRYING TO LOCK HIM UP IN THE BEDROOM! WELL, THAT LOWERED THE RESPECT THE PEOPLE HAD FOR THE PASTOR AND HIS MINISTRY WAS NEVER THE SAME AGAIN.

ANOTHER PASTOR WAS RECENTLY SACKED BY A CHURCH BECAUSE THE WIFE USED HER TONGUE, MANNERS AND JEALOUSY TO DRIVE MEMBERS AWAY. IN FACT, THAT IS THE FOURTH CHURCH THE PASTOR WILL BE SACKED BECAUSE OF THE WIFE. TOO MANY WIVES OF PASTORS HAVE MADE NEGATIVE IMPACTS UPON THEIR HUSBANDS' MINISTRY AS A RESULT OF WRONG INFLUENCE. THE WORK HAS MOVED TO A CRAWLING STAGE BECAUSE THEY HAVE BECOME THE CONDUIT PIPE FOR THE DEVIL TO INCAPACITATE THEIR HUSBANDS.

ELEVEN KINDS OF PASTOR'S WIFE TODAY

IN MY INTERACTION WITH PASTORS OF VARIOUS DENOMINATIONS, I HAVE COME TO DISCOVER VARIOUS KINDS OF PASTORS' WIVES. TAKE A CLOSE

LOOK AT THEM:

1.   THE PARASITE:

SHE IS POSSESSED BY A PARASITE SPIRIT - FEEDING ON THE HUSBAND WITHOUT CONTRIBUTING ANYTHING. SHE IS IGNORANT OF HER ROLE, BUT CLINGS TIGHTLY TO THE PASTOR. SHE IS NOT CONTRIBUTING TO THE MINISTRY BUT LOVES TO ENJOY THE REWARDS OF THE MINISTRY. SHE IS ALOOF AND SEES NOTHING GOOD IN THE WORK, BUT MAKES LOTS OF DEMAND FROM THE HUSBAND. SHE DOESN'T CARE WHERE THE HUSBAND GETS THE MONEY, SO LONG HE MEETS HER NEEDS.

2.   THE CHAMELEON:

SHE POSSESSES CHAMELEON'S NATURE. SHE HAS NO STAND OF HER OWN, BUT EASILY CHANGED BY HER ENVIRONMENT. SHE CANNOT BE PREDICTED. SHE IS A HYPOCRITE. SHE PROJECTS WHO SHE IS NOT. SHE IS ONLY INTERESTED IN CHANGING HER CLOTHS, BANGLES, GOLD AND JEWELRIES. SHE DRESSES GAITLY TO CHURCH ALL THE TIME IN LATEST ATTIRES AND FASHION, EVEN THOUGH SHE IS ROTTEN AND DEAD SPIRITUALLY. SHE PRETENDS TO BE BORN AGAIN, WHEN ACTUALLY, SHE DOESN'T KNOW THE LORD.

3.   THE PRINCIPALITY AND POWER:

SHE DOMINATES THE HUSBAND AND PUSHES HIM TO DO EVIL. SHE IS THE JEZEBEL OF NOW (I KINGS 21:4-8,25). SHE NAGS, COMPLAINS AND TAKES ACTIONS

THAT DESTROY THE IMAGE OF THE HUSBAND. SHE IS THE HUSBAND WHILE THE HUSBAND IS THE WIFE. HER STRONG PERSONALITY MAKES HER TO BULLDOZE HER WAY THROUGH EVERYWHERE.

4.   THE THUMB SUCKER:

A THUMB SUCKER IS THE WIFE THAT HAS REFUSED TO GROW UP. SHE IS IMMATURE AND ALWAYS SEES THINGS FROM HER NARROW ANGLE ONLY. SHE DEMANDS FOR ATTENTION, CARE AND NOURISHMENT ALL THE TIME. SHE COMPLAINS AND CRY ALL THE TIME, WALLOWING IN SELF-PITY.

5.   THE GARBAGE COLLECTOR:

SHE IS MOVING HERE AND THERE, PICKING STORIES, RUMORS AND A TALE BEARER. SHE IS LOOSE WITH HER MOUTH AND CAN NEVER KEEP QUIET. SHE HAS MADE LOTS OF ENEMIES WITH HER TONGUE AND IS VERY LOUSY, LOUD AND SHALLOW. SHE HAS LOST ALL RESPECT THROUGH HER RUMOR MONGERING AND TALE-BEARING ANTICS.

6.   THE WET-BLANKET:

SHE IS ALWAYS MOODY, STONE-FACED AND UNSMILING. SHE WEARS HER PROBLEMS IN HER FACE AND IS ALWAYS NEGATIVE. SHE IS FULL OF DOUBTS, WORRY, ANXIETY AND UNBELIEF. SHE SEES NO FUTURE IN THE MINISTRY AND MURMUR ALL THE TIME ABOUT UNMET NEEDS AND EXPECTATIONS. SHE HOLDS BITTERNESS AND UNFORGIVING SPIRITS WITHIN HER. NO WONDER THE DEVIL ATTACKS HER

REPEATEDLY.

7.   THE TSUNAMI:

SHE IS VOLATILE AND HAS HIGH TEMPERS. SHE IS STUBBORN, REBELLIOUS AND WOULD NOT LISTEN TO ANYONE. WHEN SHE IS ANGRY, SHE CLEARS EVERYTHING IN HER PATH, CAN HOLD GRUDGES FOR MONTHS AND SHE IS READY TO DESTROY IN A MINUTE WHAT HAS TAKEN HER YEARS TO BUILD. SHE IS MEAN AND MERCILESS WHEN SHE IS ANGRY.

8.   THE SPONGE:

SHE IS A TAKER, NOT A GIVER. SHE TAKES EVERYTHING AND SOAK THEM. SHE MAKES NO CONTRIBUTION TO THE WORK. SHE SITS AT A CORNER AND DEMANDS FOR RESPECT, HONOUR AND GIFTS, BUT WILL NOT GIVE ANY IN RETURN. SHE WILL NOT DEVELOP NOR GROW HERSELF TO GIVE AND HELP OTHERS, ONLY TO TAKE.

9.   THE TEMPTRESS:

SHE IS A SLAVE OF HER FEELINGS. SHE IS SEXUALLY ACTIVE AND WILL GIVE HERSELF TO MEN IF HER HUSBAND CANNOT SATISFY HER. SHE SEDUCES MEN IN THE CHURCH. SHE USES HER LUSTFUL HEART AND BODY TO KILL OFF THE SPIRITUAL LIFE OF THE HUSBAND THROUGH EXCESSIVE SEXUAL ACTIVITY. SHE IS AN AGENT OF SATAN SENT TO DESTROY MEN THROUGH SEX.

10. THE SERPENT:

SHE IS DEMONIC AND SATANIC. SHE IS AN AGENT OF DESTRUCTION. SHE IS DEMONIZED AND USES HER DEMONIC POWERS TO DESTROY THE WORK, FINANCES AND EFFORTS OF THE HUSBAND. SHE USES HER DEMONIC COVENANTS AND TOOLS TO RENDER THE HUSBAND IMPOTENT PHYSICALLY, SPIRITUALLY AND MINISTERIALLY.

11. THE SUNSHINE:

SHE IS A PARAGON OF GODLINESS, MATURITY AND SUBMISSIVENESS. SHE IS A PRAISE AND GLORY TO HER HUSBAND. SHE BRINGS PROGRESS, FRUITFULNESS AND ALL ROUND BLESSINGS TO THE HUSBAND THROUGH HER PRAYERS, GODLY EXAMPLES AND SUPPORT. SHE BRINGS PEACE AND REST OF MIND TO THE HUSBAND. HER HUSBAND TRUSTS HER AND CALLS HER BLESSED.

TEN OUT OF THESE NUMBERS HAVE BROUGHT NEGATIVE IMPACTS TO THE LIVES AND WORK OF THEIR HUSBANDS. THE MORE REASON MANY PASTORS ARE STRUGGLING IN MINISTRY AND FINDING THINGS TOUGH TODAY. THE MORE REASON SEPARATION AND DIVORCE HAS INCREASED GREATLY AMONG MINISTERS OF THE GOSPEL. IF YOU ARE NOT A GOOD WIFE TO HIM, GOD WILL JUDGE YOU NOW AND LATER. YOU CAN DIE OR BE DISEASED, IF YOU

PITFALLS TO AVOID AS A MINISTER'S WIFE

I READ THE STORY OF A WOMAN THAT DIED AND THE HUSBAND WAS SECRETLY HAPPY. HOWEVER, AT HER FUNERAL, THE PALLBEARERS DANCED WITH THE COFFIN AND HIT A WALL AND THE WOMAN CAME BACK TO LIFE. THE HUSBAND WAS VERY UPSET! SEVEN YEARS LATER, THE WOMAN DIED AGAIN AND AT THE FUNERAL, THE HUSBAND STERNLY WARNED THE PALLBEARERS NOT TO DANCE, BUT PUT HER GENTLY IN THE GRAVE, LEST SHE COME BACK TO LIFE AGAIN. BECAUSE, THE LAST SEVEN YEARS HAVE BEEN THE MOST TERRIBLE YEARS OF HIS LIFE AS HE SUFFERED MUCH IN THE HAND OF THE WIFE.

OBVIOUSLY, THIS WIFE FAILED TO NOTE AND AVOID THE PITFALLS OF MARRIAGE TO A MINISTER AND THE HUSBAND WAS HAPPY TO

45

SEE HER DEAD! THERE ARE MANY PITFALLS THAT A PASTOR'S WIFE MUST AVOID, IF SHE IS GOING TO BE THE NOBLE WIFE AND WOMAN GOD CREATED HER TO BE. PITFALLS ARE TRAPS AND CAREFULLY DUG HOLES THAT SWALLOW THE CARELESS AND CAREFREE PERSON. THEY PUT AN END TO AN OTHERWISE PROMISING LIFE, CAREER AND MINISTRY. IT WILL TAKE DISCIPLINE, CHANGE, PRAYERS AND WATCHFULNESS FOR YOU TO AVOID THE PITFALLS THAT ABOUND IN THE WAYS OF A MINISTER'S WIFE.

LOTS OF MINISTERS' WIVES HAVE UNWITTINGLY FALLEN INTO THE PIT AND FIND IT VERY DIFFICULT TO COME OUT. IF YOU DON'T WANT TO BECOME ANOTHER VICTIM, THEN NOTE AND WORK AGAINST THE PITFALLS I'M GOING TO ENUMERATE IN THE NEXT FEW PAGES.

Most of the marital challenges that women ascribe to the enemy are simply the outcome of their pride, rebellion, disobedience and stubbornness to their husbands.

1. PRIDE AND DISRESPECT

MANY WOMEN HAVE HARD TIME SUBMITTING TO THEIR OWN HUSBANDS. THEY ARE PROUD OF THEIR FACE, GRACE, PACE, RACE, STATE AND BODIES, THEREFORE THEY DISOBEY THEIR HUSBANDS AND DISRESPECT THEM. THAT IS A PIT THAT MANY MINISTERS' WIVES HAVE FALLEN INTO. WHEN YOU

DISRESPECT A MAN REPEATEDLY, THEN THAT MAN WILL STOP LOVING YOU. EVERY MAN WANTS RESPECT, MOST ESPECIALLY FROM HIS WIFE. BUT WHEN YOU FAIL TO GIVE IT TO YOUR HUSBAND, THEN EXPECT THE WORSE FROM HIM. PRIDE, STUBBORNNESS, ARGUING AND COMPETING WITH HIM IN WHATEVER FORM AND FOR WHATEVER REASON CAN NEVER PAY YOU. UNTIL YOU LEARN SUBMISSION AND RESPECT TO YOUR HUSBAND, YOUR MARRIAGE WILL NEVER BE STABLE AND YOU CANNOT HAVE PEACE OF MIND.

WOMEN THAT FALL INTO THIS TRAP HAVE BECOME SINGLE PARENTS, DIVORCEES AND ABANDONED TO THEIR PRIDE. WHEN YOU ARE TOO PROUD TO BE OBEDIENT TO YOUR HUSBAND, GOD'S BLESSING WILL BE FAR AWAY FROM YOU. THIS IS A PIT THAT MANY WOMEN HAVE FALLEN INTO AND THEY HAVE BEEN RUINED. MOST OF THE MARITAL CHALLENGES THAT WOMEN ASCRIBE TO THE ENEMY ARE SIMPLY THE OUTCOME OF THEIR PRIDE, REBELLION, DISOBEDIENCE AND STUBBORNNESS TO THEIR HUSBANDS. WHEN YOU DISRESPECT YOUR HUSBAND, THINGS WILL GO HAYWIRE FOR YOU.

> *"Israel hath cast off the thing that is good: the enemy shall pursue him."*
>
> - HOSEA 8:3.

2.   OVER-COMMITMENT TO CAREER OR MINISTRY

I HAVE ALREADY NOTED THAT OVER 80% OF MINISTERS' WIVES WORK OUTSIDE THE CHURCH. THEY HAVE CAREERS THAT FETCH THEM MONEY AND THEY CONTRIBUTE THAT TO THE FAMILY BUDGET. SOME MINISTERS' WIVES ARE ALSO INVOLVED IN THE MINISTRY. THEY HAVE RECEIVED CALLINGS AS EVANGELISTS, PASTORS, PROPHETESSES AND WOMEN LEADERS. UNFORTUNATELY, MANY OF THEM FALL INTO THE PIT OF BEING TOO COMMITTED TO THEIR CAREERS OR MINISTRIES AND LEAVE THE HOME AND THEIR HUSBANDS AT THE MERCY OF WOMEN PREDATORS.

WHEN YOU ARE OVER-COMMITTED, YOU GO OUT IN THE MORNING AND COME BACK LATE AT NIGHT. YOU SOMETIME GO FOR ONE OR TWO MONTHS AWAY FROM HOME AND LEAVE YOUR HUSBAND AT THE MERCY OF MAIDS AND HOUSEHELPS. SOMETIMES, YOUR OVER-COMMITMENT MEANS YOU CANNOT BE IN CHURCH MOST OF THE WEEK AND ON SUNDAY WHEN YOU ARE AROUND, YOU ARE TOO TIRED TO PARTAKE IN ANY MEANINGFUL MINISTRY. YOU ARE ALSO IN A HURRY TO GET HOME SO AS TO PREPARE FOR YOUR WORK THAT RESUMES EARNESTLY ON MONDAY MORNING.

I HAVE SEEN MANY PASTORS' WIVES WHO ARE OVER-COMMITTED TO THEIR MINISTRY AND THEY HAVE NO TIME FOR THEIR HUSBANDS, CHILDREN AND HOME. THEY KEPT THE VINEYARD OF OTHERS, BUT THEIR OWN VINEYARD HAS OVERGROWN WITH GRASS AND REPTILES.

Look not upon me, because I am black, because

the sun hath looked upon me: my mother's children were angry with me; they made me the keeper of the vineyards; but mine own vineyard have I not kept."

- SONGS OF SOLOMON 1:6.

THAT IS A GRAVE MISTAKE YOU MUST AVOID AT ALL COST, BECAUSE THE CONSEQUENCES ARE ALWAYS UNPALATABLE.

3. COMPARISON

"For we dare not make ourselves of the number, or compare ourselves with some that commend themselves: but they measuring themselves by themselves, and comparing themselves among themselves, are not wise."

- II COR. 10:12.

LOTS OF PASTORS' WIVES ARE IN THE HABIT OF COMPARING THEIR HUSBANDS WITH OTHER MEN. THEY TELL THEIR HUSBANDS, 'LOOK, YOU ARE NOT LIKE THAT PASTOR WHOSE CHURCH IS GROWING'. 'PLEASE DO SOMETHING; OR IS THAT HOW YOUR FRIEND TREAT HIS WIFE?' SUCH COMPARISONS ARE GRAVE ERRORS. THEY PUT UNNECESSARY PRESSURE ON THE MAN AND MANY TIMES LEAD THEM TO MISBEHAVE.

A PASTOR'S WIFE TOLD THE HUSBAND TO DO SOMETHING ABOUT THE CHURCH BECAUSE HIS CHURCH WAS NOT GROWING LIKE THAT OF HIS FRIENDS. WELL, THE PASTOR WENT FOR OCCULTIC POWER TO BOOST THE GROWTH OF HIS CHURCH.

ON GETTING TO THE CHURCH TO USE THE DIABOLICAL POWER AS HE WAS TOLD, THERE WAS A CHAIN REACTION AND THE PASTOR BECAME MENTALLY DERANGED FOR MORE THAN THREE YEARS. WHEN HE CAME BACK TO HIS SENSES AFTER MUCH PRAYERS FROM THE BODY OF CHRIST, HE SOLD HIS CHURCH, DIVORCED THE WIFE AND MOVED TO ANOTHER CITY TO RE-START HIS MINISTRY. THAT IS THE EVIL THAT UNGODLY COMPARISON CAN DO TO A PASTOR.

WHEN YOU CONSTANTLY NAG AND COMPLAIN ABOUT YOUR HUSBAND, THEN YOU WILL PUSH HIM TO DO STUPID AND FOOLISH THINGS THAT WILL HAVE BANDWAGON EFFECT, BOTH ON HIM AND YOU TOO!

4. BITTERNESS AND UNFORGIVING SPIRIT

Bitterness and unforgiving spirit will open you up to demonic attacks

MANY MINISTERS' WIVES ARE BITTER AGAINST THEIR HUSBANDS. THEY COMPLAIN OF LACK OF CARE AND MONEY, FORGETTING THAT BEING A GOSPEL MINISTER DOESN'T GO WITH PROSPERITY AND UNENDING FLOW OF MONEY AND MATERIAL THINGS. BEING A MINISTER IS NOT A CALLING TO AMASS WEALTH AND LIVE OSTENTATIOUSLY AND EXTRAVAGANTLY. YET, IT IS ALSO NOT A CALLING TO POVERTY AND PENURY. THE BALANCE IS THAT MINISTERS ARE CALLED TO LIVE SIMPLY AND MODERATELY. EVEN WHERE GOD SEEMS TO FAVOUR AND BLESS THEM WITH MATERIAL

THINGS, THEY ARE EXPECTED TO GIVE THEM AWAY TO THE NEEDY, LESS-PRIVILEGED AND WIDOWS.

HOWEVER, MANY PASTORS' WIVES FAIL TO SEE THIS TRUTH AND ARE THEREFORE BITTER AGAINST THEIR HUSBANDS. THEY RESENT HIS CALLING, PUT UP UNBECOMING AND NON-CHALLANT ATTITUDES TOWARDS HIS MINISTRY AND GENERALLY REFUSE TO COOPERATE AND SUPPORT HIS LITTLE EFFORTS IN MINISTRY. THIS IS ALSO A PITFALL FOR MANY PASTORS' WIVES.

BITTERNESS AND UNFORGIVING SPIRIT WILL OPEN YOU UP TO DEMONIC ATTACKS LIKE SICKNESSES, DISEASES AND CALAMITIES. YOUR BAD ATTITUDES WILL ALLOW THE DEVIL TO BUFFET THE FAMILY AND SUFFERINGS WILL BE UNRELENTING. ONCE YOU ARE MARRIED TO A MAN OF GOD, FORGIVE HIS IDIOCYCRAZINESS AND DON'T ALLOW BITTERNESS IN YOUR HEART TOWARDS HIM. COOPERATE AND SUPPORT HIM AND YOU NEVER KNOW WHAT GOD WILL DO TO REWARD YOU.

5. DEMONIZATION

I HAVE KNOWN AND SEEN MANY WIVES OF PASTORS BECOMING DEMONIZED FOR ONE REASON OR THE OTHER. BEING DEMONIZED IS HAVING A STRANGE SPIRIT THAT PUSHES YOU TO DO EVIL THINGS. IT IS THE SPIRIT OF SATAN CONTROLLING YOU FROM INSIDE. IT MAY COME DUE TO FOODS YOU EAT, INVOLVEMENT IN OCCULTIC ACTIVITIES AND A GENERATIONAL THING. YOU MAY ALSO BECOME DEMONIZED AS A RESULT OF MOVING WITH

DEMONIZED FRIENDS WHO CAMOUFLAGE AS CHRISTIANS. YOU CAN BECOME A WITCH OR WIZARD AND HAVE FAMILIAR SPIRIT OR DIVINATION SPIRIT. A DEMONIZED WOMAN IS A DANGEROUS WOMAN TO HERSELF, HER HUSBAND AND CHILDREN.

THE DEVIL LOVES TO POSSESS THE WIFE OF PASTORS SO AS TO USE THEM TO DESTROY THEIR HUSBANDS AND THEIR MINISTRY. AND LOTS OF PASTORS' WIVES HAVE FALLEN INTO THIS TRAP AS A RESULT OF TOO MUCH EATING, SLEEPING, SPIRITUAL LAZINESS, BITTER HEART AND CARELESSNESS. THE STAGNATION, CRISIS, BACKWARDNESS AND RETROGRESSION OF MINISTRY OF MANY MINISTERS CAN BE TRACED TO THEIR WIVES.

IN ONE CHURCH, THE PASTOR'S WIFE USED HER DEMONIC SPIRIT TO AFFLICT MEMBERS AND OPPRESSED THEM IN THEIR DREAMS, UNTIL EVERYBODY KNEW SHE IS THE ONE BEHIND THE SERIES OF CALAMITIES HAPPENING IN THE CHURCH. PEOPLE LEFT THE CHURCH IN DROVES. ANOTHER PASTOR'S WIFE CONFESSED DURING A DELIVERANCE SESSION THAT SHE AND OTHER DEMONIZED WOMEN IN THE CHURCH WERE THE ONES BEHIND THE POVERTY AND SQUALOR BEING EXPERIENCED BY CHURCH MEMBERS.

WELL, DEMONIZED PASTORS' WIVES ALWAYS RECEIVE CUP OF JUDGMENT FROM THE LORD, SOONER OR LATER. ONCE YOU BECOME DEMONIZED AS A PASTOR'S WIFE, YOU WILL USE THE DEMON TO DESTROY YOURSELF, YOUR HUSBAND AND YOUR CHILDREN. AND GOD WILL SEND FIERY JUDGMENT

UPON YOU. YOUR ONLY OPTION IS TO REPENT, RENOUNCE THE DEVIL AND ASK FOR DELIVERANCE PRAYERS. YOUR DEMONIZATION MAY PAY YOU FOR SOMETIME, BUT WILL DAMN YOU HERE AND HEREAFTER.

6. LONELINESS

ONE OF THE CHALLENGES A PASTOR'S WIFE HAS TO CONTEND WITH IN MINISTRY IS LONELINESS. PASTORS' WIVES DO SUFFER LONELINESS MORE, WHETHER THEIR HUSBANDS SUCCEED OR FAIL. IF THEIR HUSBAND FAIL IN MINISTRY, PEOPLE WILL ABANDON BOTH OF THEM, WHILE THE MAN MAY WITHDRAW TO HIMSELF. IF HE SUCCEEDS ON THE OTHER HAND, BECOME KNOWN AND POPULAR WITH MANY PEOPLE CRAVING FOR HIS ATTENTION, THE WIFE WILL BE ALONE AS THE HUSBAND GIVES MORE ATTENTION TO THE 'WORK OF THE LORD', LEAVING THE WOMAN TO BE ON HER OWN.

LONELINESS IS AN EMOTIONAL STATE IN WHICH A PERSON EXPERIENCES A POWERFUL FEELING OF EMPTINESS, SADNESS AND ISOLATION. IT IS A STATE OF THE HEART AND PASTORS' WIVES DO BATTLE WITH THIS FEELING OFTEN. THEY EXPERIENCE LONELINESS BECAUSE OF UNREALISTIC EXPECTATIONS FROM THEIR HUSBANDS. THEY FAIL TO RELEASE THEIR HUSBANDS UNTO THE LORD AND THEREFORE BECOME BITTER, MOODY, DEJECTED AND DEPRESSED WITH UNGODLY THOUGHTS WHEN THEY FEEL THEY ARE BEING NEGLECTED.

IT IS NOT A SIN TO FEEL LONELY BUT IT BECOMES A

SIN WHEN YOU ALLOW IT TO TAKE OVER YOUR LIFE AND PUSH YOU TO DO EVIL THINGS. THE WAY YOU HANDLE YOUR LONELINESS WILL EITHER TURN YOU TO A VIRTUOUS WOMAN OR A VIRUS. YOU ARE EITHER A GENERATOR OR A TERMINATOR BY YOUR ABILITY TO SUCCUMB OR PREVAIL OVER YOUR LONELY FEELINGS. MISHANDLING OF YOUR LONELINESS IS A PITFALL THAT HAS SWALLOWED UP MANY A MINISTER'S WIFE.

7. RELATIONSHIP WITH MALE MEMBERS

ONE OF THE ADVERSE EFFECTS OF MISHANDLING OF LONELY TIMES IS THE FACT THAT MINISTERS' WIVES WILL BEGIN TO SEEK FOR RELATIONSHIP AND ATTENTION FROM MALE MEMBERS OF THE CHURCH. INITIALLY, NO STRING IS ATTACHED, BUT GRADUALLY IT WILL TURN TO FLIRTING AND ULTIMATELY LEAD TO SEX AND SHAME. AND MANY PASTORS' WIVES HAVE FALLEN INTO THIS TRAP. THEY WILL START PLATONIC RELATIONSHIPS OF VISITING, CALLING, WELCOMING AND APPRECIATING MALE MEMBERS OF THE CHURCH. THEY WILL TAKE PARTICULAR INTERESTS IN THOSE WHO ALWAYS COMMENT ON THEIR DRESSING AND APPRECIATE THEIR COMPORTMENT.

BEFORE LONG, THERE WILL BE CRAVING FOR THOSE COMPLIMENTS AND ENJOYMENT OF THE ATTENTION THE MALE MEMBERS ARE GIVING THEM, WHICH SADLY, ARE LACKING FROM THEIR HUSBANDS. ONE THING WILL LEAD TO THE OTHER UNTIL THEY START SLEEPING WITH EACH OTHER. A PASTOR'S WIFE FELL

INTO THIS TRAP AND SHE WAS PREGNANT FOR THE ASSOCIATE PASTOR OF HER HUSBAND. ANOTHER PASTOR'S WIFE WAS PREGNANT FOR A MEMBER. ANOTHER ONE HAD A BABY EACH FOR A DEACON AND CHOIR MASTER OF THE HUSBAND'S CHURCH! WHAT AN ABOMINATION! BUT IT'S A REALITY IN TODAY'S MINISTRY.

I EVEN HEARD A FRIEND MINISTER TALKING ABOUT A GROUP OF PASTORS' WIVES INVOLVED IN LESBIANISM, AS A WAY TO RELEASE THEIR SEXUAL TENSION DUE TO THE ABSENCE OF THEIR HUSBANDS.

Pastors' wives must never fall into the trap of denying their husband their bodies, because it leads to immorality, adultery and scandals in the ministry.

THESE ARE PITFALLS THAT DESTROYED PASTORS' WIVES THEN AND NOW. GETTING INVOLVED IN RELATIONSHIPS WITH MALE MEMBERS OR WITH WOMEN WITH LESBIANISM TENDENCIES WILL ALWAYS SPELL DOOM FOR YOU, YOUR FUTURE AND FAMILY. IT IS A TRAP YOU MUST AVOID AT ALL COST.

8. WRONG ADVISERS

I HAVE SEEN, KNOWN AND HEARD OF MANY MINISTERS' WIVES THAT LOST THEIR HOME, JOY AND LIVES BECAUSE THEY LISTENED TO WRONG COUNSELS FROM BAD ADVISERS. YES, THERE IS A PLACE FOR COUNSELING IN LIFE AND MINISTRY. WE ALL

NEED GOOD ADVISES AND ADVISERS ONCE IN A WHILE. BUT IN A SITUATION WHERE THE ADVISERS ARE BADLY INFLUENCING YOU AGAINST YOUR GOD, YOUR CONSCIENCE AND HOME, IT IS BETTER TO RUN AWAY. YOUR ADVISERS CAN BE YOUR FRIENDS, CLOSE CONFIDANTS, PROPHETS, MENTORS AND LEADERS. SOME OF THEM WILL MEAN WELL, BUT SHOULD NOT BE ALLOWED TO RUIN YOUR LIFE AND HOME.

A WOMAN WAS ADVISED AND PRAYED FOR ON A MOUNTAIN BY A PROPHET THAT SHE SHOULD LEAVE HER MATRIMONIAL HOME BECAUSE HER HUSBAND DOESN'T WISH HER WELL. YET, THIS WAS A HUSBAND THAT BOUGHT A CAR FOR HER, SET HER UP IN BUSINESS AND NEVER ASKED FOR RETURNS ON THE BUSINESS. SHE LISTENED TO THE PROPHET AND MOVED OUT OF HER MARRIAGE. SHE WENT AND GOT A PLACE IN A RUN-DOWN SIDE OF THE TOWN AND SUFFERED A LOT. ONCE SHE MOVED OUT, THE HUSBAND BROUGHT IN ANOTHER WOMAN TO TAKE CARE OF HIM AND HER CHILDREN.

WELL, SHE DISCOVERED TWO YEAR LATER THAT SHE HAS BEEN DECEIVED AND WENT BACK TO BEG THE HUSBAND. BUT HE WOULD NOT BUDGE AND THAT WAS HOW SHE LOST HER HOME, KIDS AND PROSPERITY TO WRONG PROPHECIES AND ADVISERS. IF SOMEONE IS ADVISING YOU TO BE PROUD, STUBBORN AND ANTAGONIZE YOUR HUSBAND, PLEASE DON'T LISTEN, RATHER, RUN AWAY FROM SUCH BAD ADVISERS. IT IS A GREAT PITFALL THAT YOU MUST STAY VERY CLEAR AWAY FROM.

9.   DENIAL WITH SEX

VERY MANY PASTORS' WIVES USED SEX AS A WEAPON TO PUNISH AND TORMENT THEIR HUSBANDS. THE MOMENT THERE IS AN ARGUMENT, FIGHT OR MISUNDERSTANDING AND THEY ARE ANNOYED, THEY CLOSE THE 'GATE'. SOME DO IT BECAUSE THEY BELIEVED IT IS NOT FOOD AND THEIR PASTOR-HUSBAND WHO ARE HOLY MEN OF GOD SHOULD NOT BE INVOLVED IN SUCH 'CARNAL' ACTS. OTHERS ARE OF THE OPINION THAT IT SHOULD BE DONE SPARINGLY AND THAT IT WEAKENS AND REDUCES THE ANOINTING!

WELL, ALL THESE ARE MERE MYTHS AND EXCUSES THAT HOLD NO WATER. SEX BETWEEN COUPLES SHOULD BE REGULAR AS MUCH AS POSSIBLE. IT MUST NEVER BE USED AS A WEAPON TO PUNISH, REVENGE OR TORMENT EITHER PARTNER. WIVES MUST ESPECIALLY BE AVAILABLE TO THEIR HUSBANDS ALL THE TIME, EXCEPT TIME OF SICKNESS, DISEASE, DEPRESSION, TIREDNESS OR MENSTRUAL CYCLES.

PASTORS' WIVES MUST NEVER FALL INTO THE TRAP OF DENYING THEIR HUSBAND THEIR BODIES, BECAUSE IT LEADS TO IMMORALITY, ADULTERY AND SCANDALS IN THE MINISTRY. PASTORS SEE MANY WOMEN AND COUNSEL THEM EVERYDAY. THE CHURCH IS A WOMAN WORLD AND BUSINESS. AND SOME OF THESE WOMEN WOULD NOT MIND THE PASTOR SLEEPING WITH THEM! AND THEY MAY USE VARIOUS GIMMICKS, SIGN LANGUAGES AND LOTS OF TRICKS TO GET THE ATTENTION OF THE PASTOR, ESPECIALLY WHEN HE IS HIGHLY ANOINTED. TO ESCAPE SUCH INEVITABLE TEMPTATIONS, THE WIFE MUST SATISFY HER HUSBAND ALWAYS. SPOIL HIM WITH YOUR BODY AND

ONCE HE IS SATISFIED AT HOME, HE WILL NOT EAT ANY OTHER 'FRUIT' OUTSIDE, NO MATTER HOW TEMPTING AND BEAUTIFUL.

MINISTERS' WIVES THAT DENY AND MAKE THEMSELVES UNAVAILABLE TO THEIR HUSBANDS ALWAYS REGRET AND WEEP AT THE END WHEN THEY DISCOVER THE SCANDALS THAT HAVE ITS FOUNDATION IN THEIR SEXUAL DENIAL.

10. SPIRITUAL LAZINESS

YOU CANNOT BE PHYSICALLY LAZY AND EXPECT GOD TO PROSPER YOU AS MUCH AS YOU ARE SPIRITUALLY LAZY AND EXPECTING GOD'S BLESSING. BEING SPIRITUALLY LAZY MEANS YOU ARE BACKWARD IN SPIRITUAL MATTERS. LAZY IN PRAYER, READING AND STUDYING THE BIBLE, WORLDLY MINDEDNESS AND NOT BEING FERVENT IN SERVING THE LORD. IT IS TO BE MORE WISER IN SECULAR, FASHIONABLE AND CARNAL THINGS THAN IN SPIRITUAL MATTERS. AND MANY PASTORS' WIVES THAT ARE CAREER DRIVEN AND BUSINESS WOMEN FALL INTO THIS TRAP. THEY ARE NEVER THERE WHEN IT COMES TO SPIRITUAL FERVENCY. THEY CAN BARELY STRING THREE SENTENCES OF PRAYER TOGETHER AND BIBLE READING IS A BIG BURDEN TO THEM. OTHER WOMEN IN THE CHURCH ARE FAR, FAR AHEAD OF THEM WHEN IT COMES TO SPIRITUAL FERVENCY IN THE LORD, YET, THESE WOMEN COMPLAIN BITTERLY THAT THEIR HUSBANDS ARE USING OTHER WOMEN IN THE CHURCH MUCH MORE THAN THEY. THIS IS AN ERROR YOU MUST AVOID BY ALL MEANS.

PASTORS' WIVES ARE ON THE SPOTLIGHT AND

YOUR PERSONAL GROWTH AS A PASTOR'S WIFE

A CERTAIN PASTOR'S WIFE FELT THAT GOD DID NOT CALL HER, THAT ONLY HER HUSBAND IS CALLED. SHE FELT SLIGHTED AND THEREFORE DEVELOPED THE HABIT OF FIGHTING THE HUSBAND ON SATURDAY NIGHT OR SUNDAY MORNING, JUST TO DISRUPT THE SUNDAY SERVICE. SHE COULD NOT READ THE LESSON CLEARLY THE FEW TIMES SHE WAS CALLED UPON TO DO SO. THE WOMEN LEADER IN THE CHURCH WAS MUCH MORE FERVENT THAN HER AND SHE SECRETLY RESENTED HER. ONE DAY, MATTERS CAME TO A HEAD AND THE PASTOR'S WIFE SLAPPED HER IN THE PRESENCE OF CHURCH MEMBERS. THAT WAS THE END OF WOMEN FELLOWSHIP IN THAT CHURCH, BECAUSE THE WOMEN LEADER MOVED AWAY AND MAJORITY OF THE OTHER WOMEN

FOLLOWED HER.

WELL, THAT PASTOR'S WIFE BEHAVED IN SUCH AN INGNOBLE WAY BECAUSE SHE SERIOUSLY LACKED MATURITY WHICH CAN ONLY COME TO HER THROUGH PERSONAL GROWTH AND DEVELOPMENT. WHEN YOU FAIL TO DEVELOP AND WORK ON YOURSELF, YOU WILL REMAIN BACKWARD IN YOUR LIFE AND IN EVERY OTHER AREAS. BEING A GOOD PASTOR'S WIFE IS MUCH MORE THAN BEARING THE NAME, GIVING BIRTH TO CHILDREN OR SITTING DOWN TO ISSUE AUTHORITY AND COMMAND TO OTHERS. RATHER, IT INVOLVES SERIOUS PERSONAL GROWTH ON YOUR PART. YOU MUST WORK ON YOURSELF VERY WELL, ELSE YOU WILL BE ABANDONED.

BARRIERS TO BEING AN EFFECTIVE PASTOR'S WIFE

I'M AWARE OF MANY WIVES OF PASTORS WHOSE HEART CRY IS THAT THEY WANT TO BE OF IMMENSE HELP TO THEIR HUSBANDS, BUT THEY ARE BEING HAMPERED BY BARRIERS. BARRIERS ARE OBSTRUCTIONS, BULWARKS AND BARRICADES THAT MAKE PROGRESS AND ADVANCEMENT VERY DIFFICULT. THEY CAN BE SELF-IMPOSED, INHERITED OR STRATEGY OF THE DEVIL TO KEEP YOU DOWN AND BACKWARD. HOWEVER, ONE GOOD WAY TO OVERCOME THEM IS TO FIRST IDENTIFY YOUR OWN SPECIFIC BARRIERS AND WORK ROUND THEM.

LOTS OF MINISTERS' WIVES FIND BEING GOOD WIVES

DIFFICULT BECAUSE OF THE
FOLLOWING BARRIERS:

A.   PERSONAL LIMITATION
     - EDUCATIONAL,
     FAMILY, INTERNAL
     AND EXTERNAL
     LIMITATIONS.
B.   INSECURITY - FEELING
     OF JEALOUSY, ENVY
     AND BEING ANGRY AT
     OTHERS' PROGRESS.
C.   POOR BACKGROUND -
     YOUR BACKGROUND
     HAVE THE POWER TO PUT YOUR BACK ON THE
     GROUND.
D.   INFERIORITY COMPLEX - THE MINDSET THAT
     YOU ARE NOT WORTHY TO BE A PASTOR'S
     WIFE AND YOU ACCEPT IT SO.
E.   POOR ATTITUDES - THE NATURAL
     INCLINATION TO BE TOUCHY, IRRITATING,
     CRITICAL AND SARCASTIC OF YOUR HUSBAND.
F.   NO TRAINING - YOU WERE NEVER TOLD NOR
     COACHED ON HOW TO BE A GOOD
     PASTOR'S WIFE. EVERYTHING YOU DO IS BY
     TRIAL AND ERROR BASIS.
G.   BAD EXAMPLE BY LADY MINISTERS - PICKING
     UP THE WRONG COUNSEL AND ACTIONS OF
     POPULAR FEMALE MINISTERS AND ACTING
     THEM OUT IN YOUR HOME.
H.   LACK OF PERSONAL GROWTH - THE FAILURE TO
     IMPROVE AND WORK ON YOURSELF, RATHER
     YOU ARE BLAMING OTHERS FOR YOUR

To develop yourself means to work on yourself, invest seriously on personal improvement and never taking yourself for granted

PROBLEMS.

I BELIEVE THAT THE MOTHER OF ALL THESE BARRIERS IS LACK OF PERSONAL GROWTH. WHEN YOU FAIL TO GROW, IMPROVE AND DEVELOP YOURSELF, THE OTHER SEVEN BARRIERS WILL DOMINATE YOUR HEART AND LIFE, THEREBY BARRICADING YOUR UPLIFTMENT AND PROMOTIONS.

DEVELOP YOURSELF

TO DEVELOP YOURSELF MEANS TO WORK ON YOURSELF, INVEST SERIOUSLY ON PERSONAL IMPROVEMENT AND NEVER TAKING YOURSELF FOR GRANTED; IT IS THE ABILITY TO LIFT UP YOURSELF FROM NOTHING TO SOMETHING. WOMEN IN CONTEMPORARY HISTORY WHO HAVE DONE MIGHTY THINGS FOR THE LORD POSSESSED THIS ATTRIBUTE IN NO SMALL MEASURE. MENTION COULD BE MADE OF CATHERINE BOOTH, CATHERINE KHULMAN, ELIZABETH DABNEY AND SUSANNAH WESLEY.

TO WORK ON YOURSELF MEANS YOU STOP BLAMING OTHERS FOR YOUR MISFORTUNE, BITTERNESS AGAINST GOD FOR MAKING YOU A WOMAN AND TO STOP RELYING ONLY ON SUSTENANCE AND SURVIVAL. NO MATTER WHO YOU ARE, WHERE YOU ARE AND WHAT YOU WANT TO DO IN LIFE, IF YOU DON'T DEVELOP YOURSELF, YOU CANNOT REALLY AMOUNT TO ANYTHING IN LIFE. IF YOU DON'T INVEST IN YOURSELF, NOBODY WILL INVEST IN YOU. THESE ARE SOME OF THE AREAS TO DEVELOP AND WORK ON:

1.   YOUR INNER PERSON

YOU MUST WORK ON YOUR SPIRITUAL PERSON, AND BE RENEWED IN THE SPIRIT OR MIND" (EPH. 4:23). AS A PASTOR'S WIFE, DON'T AGREE TO BE PHYSICALLY OKAY BUT SPIRITUALLY, A WEAKLING. YOU MUST KNOW THE LORD INTIMATELY. BE CLOSE TO GOD IN YOUR PRAYER LIFE. BE FILLED WITH THE SPIRIT AND GODLY WISDOM. DEVELOP YOUR INNER MAN TO BE STRONG AND VIBRANT. LET YOUR INNER STRENGTH BE SUCH THAT YOU CAN HANDLE EVERY SITUATION IN A MATURED AND ADMIRABLE WAY. YOU MUST BE BIGGER WITHIN THAN WITHOUT IF YOU HOPE TO MAKE IT THROUGH THE CHALLENGES OF PASTORAL MINISTRY.

2.   COMMUNICATION ABILITY

WORK ON YOUR ABILITY TO COMMUNICATE AND SHARE WITH OTHERS. KNOW HOW TO CONVEY AND PASS YOUR MIND ACROSS TO OTHERS. LEARN TO SPEAK IN A WAY THAT PEOPLE WILL UNDERSTAND YOU. DON'T BE A RECLUSE, AN INTROVERT. YOU CANNOT SUCCEED AS A MINISTER'S WIFE LIKE THAT. DON'T ALLOW ANGER AND BITTERNESS TO CLOUD YOUR REASONING AND COMMUNICATION ABILITY. LEARN TO OPEN YOUR MOUTH IN A SIMPLE, CLEAR, COURTEOUS AND CONSISTENT WAY.

3.   EDUCATION

IF YOU HAVE NOT GONE TO FORMAL SCHOOL, GO TO AN INFORMAL AND NON-FORMAL SCHOOLS. SEEK TO BE CURRENT AND INFORMED. POLISH YOUR ENGLISH AND KNOWLEDGE. BE ENLIGHTENED AND AWARE OF THINGS AROUND YOU. DON'T BE A DULLARD AND AN IGNORAMUS. DON'T BE ASHAMED

TO LEARN, ASK QUESTIONS, READ AND STUDY, THEREBY DEVELOPING YOURSELF.

4.   RELATIONSHIPS

YOU MUST BE ABLE TO RELATE WITH VARIOUS KINDS OF PEOPLE. YOUR RELATIONAL ABILITY WILL EITHER LIFT YOU UP OR PUT YOU DOWN. YOUR RELATIONAL SKILL WILL HELP OR HINDER YOUR MARRIAGE, WORK, MINISTRY, CHILDREN AND FUTURE. WORK ON YOUR ABILITY TO RELATE WELL WITH THOSE CLOSEST TO YOU AND PEOPLE AROUND YOU. BUILD BRIDGES ACROSS TO PEOPLE AND STOP ERECTING WALLS AROUND YOURSELF. YOUR RELATIONAL SKILLS WILL EITHER DRAW PEOPLE TO YOU OR DRIVE THEM AWAY FROM YOU.

5.   SPIRITUAL GIFTS

WORK ON YOUR SPIRITUAL GIFTS. AS YOUR HUSBAND GROWS UP AND GOES UP IN MINISTRY, DON'T SIT DOWN AND BE CONTENTED WITH AVERAGE. IF YOU SIT DOWN WITHOUT DEVELOPING YOURSELF, YOU WILL BE LEFT FAR BEHIND AND THAT IS DANGEROUS FOR YOUR LIFE, MARRIAGE AND FUTURE. IF YOUR HUSBAND IS OPERATING AT 10,000 METERS HEIGHT, STRIVE TO BE BETWEEN 5-7 THOUSAND METERS. THERE IS SOMETHING IN YOU THAT THE WORLD IS WAITING FOR. TAKE TIME TO STUDY YOURSELF, DISCOVER AND DEVELOP THE GIFTS GOD HAS GRACIOUSLY GIVEN TO YOU TO BLESS YOUR

It is important that you keep adding value to yourself as a minister's wife.

WORLD. IT IS YOUR GIFTS THAT WILL OPEN DOORS FOR YOU AND BRING YOU HONOUR. IF YOU FAIL TO DEVELOP YOUR GIFTS THROUGH PRAYERS, PRACTICE AND SEIZING OPPORTUNITIES, THEY WILL LAY DORMANT AND USELESS.

6.   PHYSICAL HEALTH

DEVELOPING YOUR PHYSICAL SELF SIMPLY MEANS TAKING GOOD CARE OF YOURSELF. YOUR BODY IS THE VEHICLE THAT CARRIES YOUR SPIRIT. WITHOUT YOUR BODY, YOU ARE POWERLESS AND USELESS. LACK OF GOOD CARE OF YOUR BODY WILL RESULT IN PHYSICAL DISABILITY OR PREMATURE DEATH. AND MANY MINISTERS' WIVES HAVE DIED DUE TO ACUTE STRESS, INACTIVITY AND OVER-WEIGHT. WATCH YOUR HEALTH, EAT WELL AND ENGAGE IN REGULAR EXERCISE. STOP OVERWORKING YOURSELF AND TAKE A DERSERVED REST NOW AND THEN. TAKE REGULAR BATH AND KEEP YOUR UNDERWEARS CLEAN AND TIDY. DRESS NEATLY, SMARTLY AND MODERATELY. KEEP YOURSELF PRIME, HEALTHY AND VIBRANT AS A WOMAN OF HONOUR.

BENEFITS OF DEVELOPING YOURSELF

THERE ARE MANY BENEFITS THAT ACCRUE TO THOSE WOMEN THAT DECIDED AND DETERMINED TO IMPROVE THEMSELVES. SOME OF THE BENEFITS ARE: THOU SHALT NOT BE TAKEN FOR GRANTED; THOU SHALT BECOME RELEVANT AND MARKETABLE; THOU SHALT HAVE CONFIDENCE AND GOOD IMAGE; THOU SHALT NOT BE RELEGATED TO THE BACKGROUND;

THOU SHALT BE A GOOD MODEL AND AN EXAMPLE FOR OTHERS; THOU SHALT BE A SUCCURER OF MANY; THOU SHALT BE A VIRTUOUS WOMAN TO YOUR HUSBAND; THOU SHALT BE CALLED BLESSED BY YOUR FAMILY AND THY LIGHT SHALL SHINE TO MANY PEOPLE AND THROUGH YOUR LIGHT, MANY SHALL BE LIGHTED.

MY WIFE, KEMI, IS A VERY GOOD EXAMPLE OF PERSONAL DEVELOPMENT. FOR THE FIRST FEW YEARS OF OUR MINISTRY, MANY PASTORS THAT ATTENDED OUR CONFERENCES WERE CURIOUS AS TO WHY MY WIFE WAS ALWAYS IN THE BACKGROUND AND I DIDN'T BRING HER TO THE FRONT ALTAR. WELL, SHE WAS BUSY PRAYING, STUDYING, HONING AND IMPROVING HERSELF. IN THOSE EARLY YEARS, I FELT SHE WAS NOT RIPE ENOUGH TO FACE THE CHALLENGE OF MINISTERING TO LEADERS THEN AND SHE AGREED WITH ME. THOUGH IT WAS TOUGH, BUT SHE KEPT WORKING ON HER SKILLS, ABILITIES, CHARACTERS, SPIRITUAL AND MINISTERIAL DYNAMISM. WHEN I FELT SHE IS RIPE ENOUGH, I GRADUALLY STARTED BRINGING HER UP. HER MINISTRATIONS RECEIVED WIDE ACCLAIM AND SOME CAME TO ME ASKING WHY I HAVE NOT BEEN

SKILLS TO BE A MATURED MINISTER'S WIFE

A HIGHLY ANOINTED PASTOR TRAVELED OUT OF TOWN AND LEFT THE CHURCH WITH HIS ASSOCIATE MINISTERS, WHILE THE WIFE WAS ALSO AT HOME. IT SO HAPPENED THAT THE ASSOCIATE PASTORS WERE NOT AROUND ONE EVENING WHEN A SICK CHILD WAS BROUGHT TO THE CHURCH. THE PASTOR'S WIFE LAMENTED THAT HER HUSBAND AND THE ASSOCIATE MINISTERS WERE NOT AROUND AND THE CHILD SHOULD THEREFORE BE TAKEN TO THE HOSPITAL. BUT THE FATHER OF THE SICK GIRL REPLIED; 'YES, WE WILL TAKE HER TO THE HOSPITAL, BUT MUMMY, YOU TOO CAN PRAY, BECAUSE YOU ARE THE CLOSEST TO THE PASTOR.' AT THAT SHE DECIDED TO PRAY. SHE PRAYED A SIMPLE PRAYER AND INSTANTLY THE SICKNESS DISAPPEARED AND THE GIRL WAS

HEALED. THE PRAYER SKILL SHE HAS DEVELOPED OVER THE YEARS SAVED THE DAY AND THE GIRL.

TO BE A TRULY MATURED AND NOBLE MINISTER'S WIFE, THERE ARE SKILLS YOU MUST DEVELOP. ONE WISE MAN SAID; 'LACK OF SKILLS KILL'. THIS IS VERY TRUE. LIFE IS SKILL AND SKILL IS LIFE. WHERE YOU ARE AND WHERE YOU WILL BE IS GOING TO BE DETERMINED BY THE SKILLS YOU POSSESS. THE DIFFERENCE BETWEEN A WOMAN ENJOYING HER MARRIAGE AND THE ONE ENDURING IT IS THE SKILLS THEY POSSESS.

> *As a pastor's wife and female minister, you have to develop many skills if you want to be a successful wife, mother, minister and child of God.*

SKILL IS A SPECIAL ABILITY, CLEVERNESS AND DEXTERITY IN DOING SOMETHING. IT COMES THROUGH CONSTANT PRACTICE. IT IS A LIFE-LONG PROCESS OF LEARNING AND HONING SKILLS THAT WILL COME HANDY IN THE JOURNEY OF LIFE AND MINISTRY. THERE IS ANOINTING AND THERE IS SKILL. THERE ARE THINGS THAT ANOINTING CANNOT DO, ONLY SKILL WILL DO THEM. AS A PASTOR'S WIFE AND FEMALE MINISTER, YOU HAVE TO DEVELOP MANY SKILLS IF YOU WANT TO BE A SUCCESSFUL WIFE, MOTHER, MINISTER AND CHILD OF GOD. SKILLFUL PEOPLE ARE NOT BORN, THEY ARE MADE. SO YOU NEED TO MAKE YOURSELF BY ACQUIRING THE FOLLOWING SKILLS:

1.   SPIRITUAL GROWTH SKILLS

YOU ARE NOT PERMITTED TO BE STUNTED SPIRITUALLY, YOU NEED TO DEVELOP AND GROW CONTINUOUSLY SPIRITUALLY. YOUR SPIRITUAL LIFE IS YOUR INSURANCE; DON'T EVER NEGLECT IT FOR WIFEHOOD, MOTHERHOOD OR MINISTRY. GOD SHOULD COME FIRST BEFORE ANY OTHER THING CAN FOLLOW (I COR. 8:2, II PET. 3:18)

2.   PRAYER SKILLS

TO DEVELOP SPIRITUAL GROWTH SKILLS, YOU MUST BE ABLE TO DEVELOP FIRE BRAND PRAYER SKILL. YOUR PRAYER LIFE MUST BE SOUND, CONSISTENT, HABITUAL AND ADDICTIVE. WITHOUT PRAYER LIFE, YOU WILL BE HELPLESS. GET UP AND PRAY; PROTECT YOURSELF, YOUR HUSBAND, CHILDREN AND MINISTRY (I COR. 4:20, JAMES 5:16)

3.   HOSPITALITY SKILL

AS A PASTOR'S WIFE OR A FEMALE MINISTER, YOU CAN'T AFFORD TO BE SNOBBISH; YOU MUST BE HOSPITABLE AND GENEROUS. YOU WILL NEED TO ATTEND TO A LOT OF VISITORS IN YOUR HOUSE; THEY MUST ALL GO WITH GOOD IMPRESSION ABOUT YOU. WELCOME YOUR VISITORS WITH SMILE, EVEN IF YOU DON'T HAVE ANYTHING TO GIVE THEM. ENTERTAIN THEM WITH JOY; IT IS A PRIVILEGE TO HAVE SOMEBODY COMING TO YOUR HOUSE. (I TIMOTHY 3:2, ROMANS 15:13, 1 PETER 4:9).

4.   DOMESTIC SKILLS

CLOSE TO THAT IS A DOMESTIC SKILL. YOU MUST BE A HOME MAKER, DON'T EVER ALLOW MINISTRY TO TAKE THAT AWAY FROM YOU. YOU MUST BE A GREAT COOK AND A GOOD ORGANIZER AT HOME. YOU MUST BE THOUGHTFUL AND WISE. YOUR CANDLE MUST NOT GO OUT IN THE NIGHT. (PROVERBS 31:18, 11:29).

5. TIME MANAGEMENT SKILL

MEN GENERALLY HATE IT WHEN THEIR WIVES ARE SLOW AND WASTE TIME. YOU MUST LEARN HOW TO MANAGE YOUR TIME WELL BECAUSE YOU ARE MANY THINGS TO MANY PEOPLE; YOU MUST KNOW HOW TO BALANCE YOUR LIFE. TO SOME; YOU ARE JUST THEIR MOTHER, TO A MAN, YOU ARE HIS WIFE, TO ANOTHER; YOU ARE THEIR COUNSELOR, TO OTHERS YOU ARE THEIR PROPHETESS. HOW WILL YOU MANAGE THESE? GET ORGANIZED, MANAGE YOUR TIME, HAVE A 'TO DO' LIST. YOU CAN ACHIEVE MORE IF YOU ORGANIZE YOURSELF.

6. RELATIONAL SKILLS

THIS IS VERY IMPORTANT, MINISTRY IS ABOUT PEOPLE, YOU MUST KNOW HOW TO HANDLE PEOPLE, YOU MUST KNOW HOW TO HANDLE ALL KINDS OF MEN AND WOMEN WITHOUT HURTING YOURSELF. HANDLE YOUR IN-LAWS WISELY, CHURCH MEMBERS, YOUR HUSBAND'S SUPERIOR LEADERS, YOUR ASSOCIATE, YOUR MENTORS, MEN AND WOMEN IN THE CHURCH, YOUTH AND SINGLES, YOU NEED TO DEVELOP YOURSELF TO DO ALL THESE (PROVERBS 15:1-2)

7.　WOMEN MANAGEMENT SKILLS

YOU NEED TO KNOW HOW TO MANAGE WOMEN IN THE CHURCH; YOU NEED TO BE WISE AND BOLD. YOU MUST KNOW HOW TO HANDLE THEIR GOSSIP, EMOTIONAL OUTBURST, INSUBORDINATION AND TEMPTATIONS, ETC.

8.　CONFLICT MANAGEMENT SKILLS

MEN ARE THE PILLARS OF THE CHURCH, WOMEN ARE THE BEAUTY OF THE CHURCH, YOUTH, SINGLES AND CHILDREN ARE THE FUTURE OF THE CHURCH. THE PRESENCE OF THESE SET OF PEOPLE WITH DIFFERENT NEEDS IN THE CHURCH WILL DEFINITELY LEAD TO CRISIS ONCE IN A WHILE, YOU MUST HAVE 'SHOCK ABSORBER', AND YOU MUST KNOW HOW TO MANAGE CONFLICT, WHICH IS INEVITABLE IN THE CONGREGATION OF MEN. (JAMES 3:16-18)

9.　MINISTRY SKILLS

YOU MUST DEVELOP SKILLS FOR THE MINISTRY EVEN IF YOU ARE A PASTOR'S WIFE WITHOUT A PERSONAL CALL INTO THE MINISTRY. SINCE YOUR HUSBAND IS CALLED, YOU MUST DEVELOP YOURSELF. YOU MUST DEVELOP YOUR TEACHING SKILLS, COUNSELING SKILLS, ETC. (II PETER 1:10)

10.　S U C C E S S   A N D   F A I L U R E MANAGEMENT SKILLS

YOU MUST KNOW HOW TO HANDLE SUCCESS WITHOUT BECOMING COCKY, PROUD OR LOSE

YOUR HEAD BECAUSE OF FAME, WEALTH AND PRAISE OF MEN. YOU MUST ALSO KNOW HOW TO HANDLE FAILURE AND CHALLENGES WITHOUT BREAKING DOWN OR CURSING GOD, YOU MUST BECOME AN ALL-ROUND PERSONALITY.

11. COMMUNICATION SKILL

MINISTRY IS ALL ABOUT COMMUNICATION AND PROBLEM SOLVING. YOU MUST KNOW HOW TO TALK TO PEOPLE WITHOUT HURTING THEM. IF YOU ARE FOND OF BEING RUDE AND ABUSIVE, PEOPLE WILL ABANDON YOU, YOUR HUSBAND AND YOUR MINISTRY (JAMES 3:5)

12. FINANCIAL MANAGEMENT SKILL

YOU MUST BE A GOOD MANAGER OF MONEY AND MATERIALS. IF YOU WANT TO GO FAR IN LIFE AND MINISTRY, YOU MUST UNDERSTAND THAT NOT ALL MONEY IS SPENDABLE. YOU MUST KNOW HOW TO MANAGE MONEY, PAY TITHES AND OFFERINGS, SAVINGS, BUDGETING, INVESTMENT AND PAYMENTS OF TAXES SO AS TO AVOID FINANCIAL MESS.

13. PARENTAL SKILLS

YOUR HUSBAND MAY NOT HAVE ENOUGH TIME TO RAISE YOUR CHILDREN; YOU MUST NOT ABANDON THEM FOR MINISTERIAL WORK. THEY ARE YOUR FIRST CHURCH. READ BOOK ABOUT MOTHERHOOD AND PARENTING, DEVELOP YOURSELF AND BE A GREAT MOTHER. (PROVERBS 13:24)

14. TECHNOLOGICAL SKILL

YOU MUST DEVELOP YOURSELF TECHNOLOGICALLY. YOU MUST BE ABLE TO USE MODERN MACHINES TO DO OLD THINGS. YOU MUST PERFECT THE USE OF COMPUTERS, GAS COOKER, MICROWAVE OVEN, WASHING MACHINE, DISH WASHER, ETC. YOU MUST UPDATE YOURSELF AND BECOME UP-TO-DATE. TO BE CORRECT; YOU MUST BE CURRENT.

15. LEADERSHIP SKILL

IF YOU ARE A FEMALE MINISTER, YOU ARE A LEADER IN THE CHURCH. IF YOU A PASTOR'S WIFE; YOU ARE A LEADER AMONG WOMEN IN YOUR CHURCH AND TO YOUR CHILDREN. YOU MUST DEVELOP LEADERSHIP SKILL. YOU MUST KNOW THAT LEADERSHIP IS NOT ABOUT DICTATORSHIP BUT ABOUT INFLUENCE. GO AHEAD AND DEVELOP YOUR LEADERSHIP ABILITY.

16. FOLLOWERSHIP ABILITY

YOU MUST BE A GOOD FOLLOWER OF YOUR HUSBAND (I COR. 11:1). YOU CAN'T BE A GOOD WIFE IF YOU ARE NOT A GOOD FOLLOWER. YOU CAN'T BE A GOOD LEADER IF YOU DON'T KNOW HOW TO FOLLOW WELL (I PETER 2:18)

17. CHARACTER DEVELOPMENT SKILL

CHARACTER IS LIFE; YOU MUST LEARN HOW TO DEVELOP WHOLESOME CHARACTER. *Deal with anger, laziness, dirtiness, gossip, hatred, oversleeping, stinginess, extravagancy, borrowing, stealing, lying, fighting, malice, abusive words, gluttony, nagging,* ETC. ALL THESE WILL

NOT ONLY DESTROY YOUR MINISTRY AND MARRIAGE; THEY CAN DESTROY YOUR LIFE. HENCE, DEVELOP GODLY CHARACTERS LIKE DILIGENCE, BOLDNESS, FORGIVENESS, MEEKNESS, OBEDIENCE, PRUDENCY AND GENEROSITY AMONG OTHERS.

18. OUTLOOK SKILL

DON'T EVER THINK BECAUSE YOUR HUSBAND IS A SPIRITUAL MAN, HE DOES NOT CARE IF YOU DRESS AND LOOK LIKE GRANDMA OR LIKE HIS MAID, NO! HE WANTS TO SEE A QUEEN IN YOU, SO DRESS NEATLY, BALANCED COLOUR, AND LOOK NEAT, NICE, TOUCHABLE AND BEAUTIFUL. HOLINESS IS NOT A SYNONYM OF DIRTINESS.

19. MATRIMONIAL SKILLS

BECOME A GREAT WIFE, BE A SUCCOR TO YOUR HUSBAND. A COMPLETER, NOT A COMPETITOR, A ROMANCER, A FRIEND, SUPPORTER, A PILLAR NOT A CATERPILLAR, A MOTHER NOT A MURDERER, A MINISTER NOT A MONSTER, A WIFE NOT A KNIFE. LET YOUR HUSBAND BE HAPPY THAT HE MARRIED YOU. TURN TO YOUR HUSBAND AND MAKE HIM HAPPY, HE SHOULD BE NUMBER ONE IN YOUR LIFE AFTER GOD, NOT YOUR CAREER, MINISTRY OR YOUR CHILDREN.

20. BEDROOM SKILLS

YOUR HUSBAND IS A SPIRITUAL MAN, BUT HE IS STILL IN THE FLESH, SO SATISFY HIM SEXUALLY. SATISFYING YOUR HUSBAND IN THE BEDROOM IS ONE OF YOUR

PASTOR'S WIFE AND MINISTRATION IN THE CHURCH

THERE HAD BEEN LOTS OF CONTROVERSIES AND PRACTICES REGARDING THE ROLE OF THE PASTOR'S WIFE IN THE CHURCH. IN THE PAST, MANY MINISTERS DID NOT RECOGNIZE THEIR WIVES IN THE MINISTRY. THEY RELEGATED THEM TO THE BACKGROUND. BUT TODAY, LOTS OF MINISTERS ARE PLACING THEIR WIVES AS CO-FOUNDERS AND CO-PASTORS IN THE CHURCH, WHETHER THEY HAVE THE CALLING AND COMPETENCE OR NOT. FURTHERMORE, THE PASTOR'S WIFE IS AUTOMATICALLY THE HEAD OF THE WOMEN MINISTRY OF THE CHURCH, WHETHER SHE HAS THE LEADERSHIP TRAITS OR NOT. IT IS TIME TO GAIN SOME VALUABLE WISDOM IN THIS REGARD.

A. MINISTRY AND SCRIPTURAL REALITIES

> *"There was in the days of Herod, the king of Judaea, a certain priest named Zacharias, of the course of Abia: and his wife was of the daughters of Aaron, and her name was Elisabeth. And they were both righteous before God, walking in all the commandments and ordinances of the Lord blameless…And it came to pass, that, as soon as the days of his ministration were accomplished, he departed to his own house. And after those days his wife Elisabeth conceived, and hid herself five months"*
>
> - LUKE 1:5-6,23-24

YES, MANY INDEPENDENT CHURCHES PRACTICE VARIOUS OPINIONS, YET WE NEED BIBLICAL BALANCE. EVEN THOUGH ZACHARIAH WAS A PRIEST, THAT DID NOT MAKE THE WIFE ONE, THOUGH SHE IS FROM THE LINEAGE AARON.

A. THE CALLING OF THE HUSBAND IS NOT THE CALLING OF THE WIFE.

B. YES, HUSBAND AND WIFE ARE ONE IN BODY, BUT SEPARATE IN SPIRIT.

C. GOD RESERVES THE RIGHT TO GIVE DIFFERENT GIFTS AND CALLING TO THE WIFE.

D. CO-FOUNDERSHIP AND CO-PASTORSHIP IS NOT SCRIPTURAL, EXCEPT GOD COMMANDS AND DIRECTS.

E. PLACING THE WIFE AUTOMATICALLY IN ANY

OF THE FIVE FOLD MINISTRY WILL LEAD TO GRAVE CONSEQUENCES.

F. FUNCTIONING WHERE GOD HAS NOT CALLED YOU WILL LEAD TO DISASTER. I KNOW A PASTOR'S WIFE THAT WAS GIFTED AS A PRAYER WARRIOR, WHO SHOULD BE INTERCEDING FOR THE HUSBAND AND THE CHURCH IN SECRET. BUT SHE WAS PLACED ON THE ALTAR AND AFTER SOME YEARS, SHE RECEIVED AN ARROW AND SHE BECAME TERRIBLY SICK. AFTER MANY MONTHS IN THE HOSPITAL, SHE DIED! THE HUSBAND LATER LEARNT THE LESSON THAT IT WAS BECAUSE OF HER UNNECESSARY ON THE ALTAR.

LOTS OF PASTORS' WIVES HAVE CONTRIBUTED MORE TO CHURCH DECLINE THAN GROWTH DUE TO THESE ERRORS. WHEN YOU ARE THRUST INTO A POSITION YOU DON'T HAVE A CALLING AND COMPETENCE FOR, YOU WILL SURELY LEAD THE WORK BACKWARD.

B. A TRUE MUMMY AND LEADER

PASTORS' WIVES FACE LOTS OF BATTLES IN THE CHURCH. THERE ARE THOSE THAT LOVE TO HATE YOU; DISDAIN YOU; FEEL YOU ARE TOO YOUNG; TOO LUCKY TO MARRY A PASTOR; UNFIT TO MARRY A PASTOR AND WISH YOU DEAD. AND THEY WILL ATTACK YOU PHYSICALLY, VERBALLY, SPIRITUALLY AND PSYCHOLOGICALLY. MANY WILL NOT ACCEPT NOR RESPECT YOU IMMEDIATELY. IT TAKES TIME TO GAIN RESPECT AND INFLUENCE. YOU MUST THEREFORE DISPLAY:

? TACT, WISDOM AND SMARTNESS.
? RESPECT AND HONOUR TO ALL.
? SPIRITUAL SAGACITY AND POWER.
? PRAYERFUL SPIRIT AND DEVOTION.
? CONTENT TO BE IN THE SHADOW OF YOUR HUSBAND.
? DIGNIFIED POSTURE AND WISE COMMUNICATIONS.
? BI-PARTISAN AND BROAD MINDEDNESS.
? SHOWING LOVE, CARE AND CONCERN FOR ALL.
? PERSONAL GROWTH, COMPETENCE AND MINISTRY-WISE.
? HOLY SPIRIT ANOINTING AND SUPERNATURAL POWER.

IT IS WHEN YOU DISPLAY THESE TRAITS THAT YOU CAN START TO EARN THE RESPECT OF THE WOMEN AND MEN IN THE CHURCH. IT IS WHEN THEY TRULY SEE SOMETHING IN YOU THAT THEY DON'T HAVE THEY WILL BEGIN TO RESPECT YOU.

C. DISCOVERING YOUR GIFTS AND CALLING.

"And he gave some, apostles; and some, prophets; and some, evangelists; and some, pastors and teachers; For the perfecting of the saints, for the work of the ministry, for the edifying of the body of Christ: Till we all come in the unity of the faith, and of the knowledge of the Son of God, unto a perfect man, unto the measure of the stature of the fullness of Christ."
- EPH. 4:11-13.

78

"Having then gifts differing according to the grace that is given to us, whether prophecy, let us prophesy according to the proportion of faith; Or ministry, let us wait on our ministering: or he that teacheth, on teaching; Or he that exhorteth, on exhortation: he that giveth, let him do it with simplicity; he that ruleth, with diligence; he that sheweth mercy, with cheerfulness."
- ROMANS 12:6-8

IT IS NOT EVERY PASTOR'S WIFE THAT IS CALLED TO THE PULPIT AND MINISTERIAL MINISTRY. YOU MUST DISCOVER WHAT GOD HAS CALLED YOU TO DO AND THE GIFTS HE HAS GIVEN YOU. FROM EXPERIENCE, SOME ARE CALLED AND GIFTED AS:

? PERSONAL EVANGELISTS.
? COUNSELORS.
? INTERCESSORS AND PRAYER WARRIORS.
? PROPHETESSES.
? CHILDREN MINISTERS.
? FINANCIAL SUPPORTERS.
? ENCOURAGERS.
? ADMINISTRATORS.
? SINGERS AND WORSHIPPERS.
? MINISTRY TO PROSTITUTES, SINGLE MOTHERS, YOUTHS, TEENAGERS, MIDWIVES, ETC.

STOP FIGHTING YOUR HUSBAND FOR THE PULPIT OR ALTAR. RATHER, BE CONTENT TO OPERATE IN THE AREA OF YOUR GIFTS. LOTS OF WOMEN HAVE MADE MUCH MORE IMPACT THROUGH THEIR GIFTS AND MINISTRIES THAN BEING PLACED ON THE ALTAR. IF GOD HAS GIVEN YOU A PRIVATE MINISTRY, DON'T SEEK FOR A PUBLIC ONE. IF YOU CAN MAKE IMPACT ON INDIVIDUAL LIVES, BE CONTENT WITH THAT

THAN BEING PLACED ON THE ALTAR WHERE YOU WILL MESS UP AND MAKE LITTLE OR NO IMPACT.

WHATEVER IS YOUR BURDEN, PASSION OR DREAMS AND YOU FIND JOY, RESULTS AND COMPETENCE IN DOING IS YOUR GIFT AND CALLING. ONCE YOU CAN DISCOVER THEM AND FOCUS ON THEM, YOU WILL BE EFFECTIVE AND RESPECTED. BIMBO ODUKOYA'S HUSBAND WAS THE ONE THAT CHOSE HER TO HANDLE TEENAGERS AND SINGLES DEPARTMENT. SHE IMPACTED THE WORLD POSITIVELY.

D. RALLYING THE WOMEN TO COMMON PURPOSE

YOUR GIFT AND CALLING SHOULD HELP YOU TO ENCOURAGE AND MENTOR OTHER WOMEN IN THE CHURCH. YOU MUST ALLOW THE WOMEN MINISTRY IN THE CHURCH TO FUNCTION EFFECTIVELY.

? DON'T BE THE LEADER, LET SOMEONE ELSE LEAD. YOU MAY START, BUT GRADUALLY HAND IT OVER TO CAPABLE WOMEN.

? YOU SHOULD BE THE MATRON THAT THEY WILL COME TO FOR ADVISE.

HOW TO MAKE HIS MINISTRY ENJOYABLE

I T IS IMPORTANT THAT EVERY PASTOR'S WIFE KNOW HOW TO MAKE THE MINISTRY OF THE HUSBAND TO PROSPER. MEN ARE MOTIVATED BY THEIR WORK, AND ONCE YOU SHOW INTEREST IN HIS WORK AND DOING YOUR PART TO MAKE IT ENJOYABLE FOR HIM, YOUR PEACE OF MIND IS GUARANTEED. PERMIT ME TO GIVE YOU SOME TIPS ALONG THIS LINE:

A.   RELATE WELL WITH CHURCH MEMBERS

RELATIONSHIP IS THE ABILITY TO GET ALONG AND GO ALONG WITH DIFFERENT KINDS OF PEOPLE. INGREDIENTS OF GOOD RELATIONSHIPS ARE SMILE, HONESTY, INTEREST, CARE, CONCERN, APPRECIATION,

81

SHARING, TRUTHFULNESS, COUNSEL AND PRAYER SUPPORT. IT IS NOT EVERYONE THAT WILL RELATE WELL WITH YOU IN THE CHURCH.

HERE ARE TYPES OF PEOPLE YOU HAVE IN ANY CHURCH:-

1. **THE PROUD** - THEY LOOK DOWN ON YOU AS THE PASTOR'S WIFE. THEY BELIEVE YOU ARE TOO SMALL TO LEAD THEM OR BE THE WIFE OF THEIR PASTOR.
2. **THE GREEN SNAKE** - THOSE WHO WANT TO MANIPULATE YOU. THEY WANT TO SUBTLY DIRECT AND CONTROL YOUR AFFAIRS.
3. **THE USER** - THOSE WHO ONLY WANT TO TAKE FROM YOU.
4. **THE BACKSTABBER** - PEOPLE WHO BACKBITE YOU TO OTHERS, THOUGH CLOSE TO YOU.
5. **THE KILLER** - THOSE WHO WANT YOU DEAD BECAUSE OF JEALOUSY AND ENVY.
6. **THE WELL-MEANING** - THOSE WHO ACCEPT AND LOVE YOU FOR WHO YOU ARE.

SOME PASTORS' WIVES RELATE WITH MEMBERS BECAUSE OF THEIR MONIES AND WHAT THEY WILL BENEFIT, BUT THEY WILL LAND YOU IN TROUBLE.

SEVEN DON'T OF RELATIONSHIP WITH MEMBERS

1. DON'T BE TOO FAMILIAR WITH CHURCH MEMBERS (TOO MUCH FAMILIARITY BREEDS CONTEMPT).
2. DON'T HAVE SKELETON IN YOUR CUPBOARD AND WASH YOUR DIRTY LINEN IN THE PUBLIC (THE FRIEND OF TODAY MAY BE THE ENEMY OF

TOMORROW).
3.   DON'T GO AND BORROW MONEY FROM CHURCH MEMBERS. (THE BORROWER IS SERVANT TO THE LENDER).
4.   DON'T HAVE SECRET DISCUSSION OF 'LET NOBODY HEAR THIS' WITH MEMBERS. (WALLS HAVE EARS).
5.   DON'T BE A SLAVE OF FOOD BY EATING EVERYWHERE (IT MAKES YOU TO LOSE RESPECT AND HONOUR).
6.   DON'T BE A TALKATIVE. (IT MAKES YOU SAY SOMETIMES WHAT YOU NEVER PLANNED TO SAY).
7.   DON'T ALLOW ANY OUTSIDER TO TAKE THE NUMBER ONE POSITION IN YOUR RELATIONAL AGENDA. (YOUR HUSBAND MUST ALWAYS BE THE NUMBER ONE).

> *Don't have hang ups and airs about you, but be simple, godly, reserved and respectful.*

IT IS TRUE THAT THERE IS NO WAY BY WHICH YOU WILL NOT BE FAMILIAR WITH CHURCH MEMBERS AS A MINISTER'S WIFE WHO CARES FOR THE SHEEP. BUT THERE MUST BE SOME LIMITS. IF NOT, PEOPLE WILL TAKE YOUR FAMILIARITY FOR STUPIDITY AND YOUR HUMILITY TO MEAN HUMILIATION.

B.   COMPORT YOURSELF WELL

YOUR COMPORTMENT AND CARRIAGE IS VERY

CRUCIAL. DRESS THE WAY YOU WANT TO BE ADDRESSED. YOU CAN'T DRESS LIKE A PROSTITUTE AND EXPECT TO BE ACCORDED THE RESPECT OF A QUEEN. COMPORT YOURSELF IN A DIGNIFIED, HONOURABLE AND RESPECTABLE WAY. DON'T HAVE HANG UPS AND AIRS ABOUT YOU, BUT BE SIMPLE, GODLY, RESERVED AND RESPECTFUL. CONDUCT YOURSELF IN A WAY THAT YOU WILL GAIN THE CONFIDENCE OF YOUR HUSBAND AND CHURCH LEADERSHIP. DON'T BE FORWARD OR DABBLE INTO MATTERS THAT YOU ARE NOT INVITED TO. BE CAUTIOUS AND CORTEOUS.

C. SHOW YOUR SUPPORT FOR HIS MINISTRY

THE FOLLOWING ARE TANGIBLE WAYS YOU CAN DEMONSTRATE YOUR SUPPORT FOR HIS MINISTRY:-

1. **NEVER SAY YOU ARE NOT CALLED BY GOD**: YOU ARE CALLED; GOD CANNOT CALL THE 'HEAD' WITHOUT CALLING THE 'BODY'. YOU ARE EITHER PASTOR'S WIFE BY BIRTH OR BY TRAINING. YOU ARE PASTOR'S WIFE BY BIRTH IF YOU KNEW BEFORE YOUR MARRIAGE THAT GOD IS CALLING YOU TO MARRY A PASTOR. YOU ARE A PASTOR'S WIFE BY TRAINING IF YOU NEVER KNEW YOUR HUSBAND WILL EVENTUALLY BECOME A PASTOR BEFORE YOU MARRY HIM. ALLOW YOURSELF TO BE TRAINED FOR IT AS SOON AS YOU KNOW AND GROW UP IN YOUR SPIRITUAL LEVEL INTO THE MINISTRY.

2. **BELIEVE IN HIM AND HIS MINISTRY**:
YOU NEED TO DO THIS, EVEN IF THERE IS NO RESULT YET. IF THERE IS NOTHING TO PROVE HE IS CALLED, JUST HOLD ON TO GOD AND YOUR HUSBAND; BELIEVE HIM, RESULT WILL COME.

"A virtuous woman is a crown to her husband: but she that maketh ashamed is as rottenness in his bones."
- PROVERBS 12:4

3. **ENCOURAGE HIM IN FAILURE, CELEBRATE HIM IN SUCCESS.**
TELL HIM IT IS WELL, STAND WITH HIM DURING CHURCH CRISIS. DEFEND, PROTECT, AND MOTIVATE HIM. WHEN HE SUCCEEDS, CELEBRATE IT NO MATTER HOW IT SEEMS, AND THEN GIVE GLORY TO GOD.

"Iron sharpeneth iron; so a man sharpeneth the countenance of his friend... As the fining pot for silver, and the furnace for gold; so is a man to his praise."
- PROVERBS 27: 17, 21

4. **KEEP SECRETS**:
NEVER REVEAL THE SECRETS OF CHURCH MEMBERS YOU ARE PRIVILEGED TO KNOW THROUGH HIM TO OTHERS. IF YOU ARE LOOSE IN DIVULGING INFORMATION TO MEMBERS, YOU WILL LOSE THEIR RESPECT.

85

5. **SUPPORT HIS LEADERSHIP/FOLLOWERSHIP**: HELP HIM TO LEAD HIS FOLLOWERS WELL, TO LOVE AND RESPECT THEM AND PAY THEM GOOD SALARY. YOU TOO SHOULD BE GENEROUS TO THESE FOLLOWERS. ALSO HELP HIM TO FOLLOW HIS LEADERS; DON'T HELP HIM TO BREAK THE CHURCH AND CARRY THE MEMBERS AWAY.

6. **SUPPORT FINANCIALLY**: PASTORS ARE KNOWN TO BE ONE OF THE MOST POORLY PAID PROFESSION IN THE WORLD. THEY CAN'T PROTEST, GO ON STRIKE OR FORM "PASTOR'S UNION" TO FIGHT FOR THEIR WAGES; THEY CAN ONLY SUFFER IN SILENCE, THEREFORE, PRAY AND TRUST GOD. MAY BE GOD PLANTED YOU INTO HIS LIFE TO COVER THIS PART OF HIS LIFE, DON'T FAIL GOD, SUPPORT FINANCIALLY.

7. **HELP RAISE YOUR CHILDREN:** YOUR HUSBAND WILL TRAVEL OFTEN AS A PASTOR, YOU NEED TO RISE UP TO RAISE YOUR CHILDREN IN THE WAY OF THE LORD IN HIS ABSENCE. GOOD CHILDREN WILL BE A PLUS TO BOTH OF YOU AND THE MINISTRY.

"The rod and reproof give wisdom: but a child left to himself bringeth his mother to shame… Correct thy son, and he shall give thee rest; yea, he shall give delight unto thy soul."
\- PROVERBS 29:15,17.

FEMALE
MINISTERS

IN THIS SECOND PART,
WE SHALL BE ADDRESSING ISSUES
THAT ARE IMPORTANT TO THE LIFE,
MINISTRY AND CHALLENGES BEING
FACED BY LADY MINISTERS TODAY.
I TRUST THE LORD TO USE IT TO
BRING CHANGE IN NEEDED AREAS.

THE FEMALE MINISTER AND MINISTRY

CATHERINE BOOTH WAS A PASTOR'S WIFE AND ALSO A WOMAN MINISTER. ACTUALLY, SHE WAS THE ONE THAT FIRST RECEIVED THE CALL TO MINISTRY BEFORE THE HUSBAND. THE HUSBAND WAS NATURALLY A SHY AND TIMID FELLOW, HOWEVER, CATHERINE WAS OUTGOING AND BOLD. SHE THEREFORE HELPED THE HUSBAND TO OVERCOME HIS TIMIDITY AND SHE EMBRACED HIS CALL. SHE TOO WORKED ALONG SIDE THE HUSBAND AND THEY BOTH LED THE CHURCH, SALVATION ARMY TOGETHER. SHE FUNCTIONED WELL, BOTH AS A PASTOR'S WIFE AND A FEMALE MINISTER. THE CHURCH SHE HELPED THE HUSBAND TO LEAD IS STILL GOING STRONG, MORE THAN 200 YEARS LATER.

YES, SOMETIMES, GOD CALLS A WOMAN BOTH TO BE A PASTOR'S WIFE AND LATER A FEMALE MINISTER. MANY WOMEN ARE FUNCTIONING IN THESE TWO ROLES VERY WELL. A SCRIPTURAL EXAMPLE IS AQUILA AND PRISCILLA. THEY WERE BOTH MENTIONED FIVE TIMES IN THE BIBLE (ACTS 18:2,18,26; ROM. 16:3; II TIM. 4:19). THE WIFE, PRISCILLA WAS MENTIONED FIRST 3 TIMES, WHILE THE HUSBAND WAS MENTIONED FIRST 2 TIMES. WHY? IT APPEARS THE WIFE HAS MORE DOMINANT GIFT AND MINISTRY THAN THAT OF THE HUSBAND.

Being a Pastor's wife does not automatically mean that you are called into Pastoral ministry.

GOD RESERVES THE RIGHT TO CALL ANYONE INTO HIS SERVICE AND SOMETIMES HE CALLS BOTH HUSBAND AND WIFE. AT OTHER TIMES, HE CALLS THE MAN AND LEAVES THE WOMAN ALONE. MOST TIMES, HE CALLS AND GIVES SPECIAL ASSIGNMENT TO THE WOMAN, DIFFERENT FROM THAT OF THE HUSBAND. FOR EXAMPLE, WHILE GOD CAN CALL THE HUSBAND INTO THE FIVE-FOLD MINISTRY, HE CAN DECIDE TO CALL THE WIFE INTO CHILDREN, YOUTH, SINGLES OR INTERCESSORY MINISTRY.

DISCOVERING YOUR CALLING

IT IS IMPORTANT THAT YOU RECEIVE YOUR PERSONAL CALL FROM THE LORD AS A FEMALE MINISTER. PEOPLE MIGHT TELL YOU THAT GOD IS CALLING YOU, THAT IS NOT ENOUGH. YOU MUST GET

PERSONAL WITH THE LORD AND HEAR FROM HIM DIRECTLY YOURSELF. THEN YOU MUST DISCOVER THE AREA HE HAS CALLED YOU TO. BEING A PASTOR'S WIFE DOES NOT AUTOMATICALLY MEAN THAT YOU ARE CALLED INTO PASTORAL MINISTRY. YOU MUST LET THE LORD CLARIFY YOUR CALL AND ASSIGNMENT IN THE VINEYARD. YOU MUST DISCOVER WHETHER HE HAS CALLED YOU TO HOLD FORTH WITH YOUR HUSBAND OR BE A LADY EVANGELIST, PROPHETESS, OR TO START A SEPARATE MINISTRY OF YOUR OWN TO WOMEN, YOUTH, COUNSELLING, CHILDREN OR WIDOWS.

THIS TRUTH CANNOT BE OVER-EMPHASIZED. I HAVE SEEN LOTS OF FEMALE MINISTERS WHO FAILED TO GET THEIR MINISTRY VERY CLEAR FROM THE LORD AND THEY ARE NOT FRUITFUL AS THEY SHOULD. DON'T FALL INTO SUCH ERROR. NOT ALL FEMALE MINISTERS ARE CALLED TO PLANT, START CHURCHES OR BE LADY PASTORS. VERY MANY ARE GIVEN ASSIGNMENTS THAT WILL FURTHER THE KINGDOM OF GOD. GET YOUR AREA OF MINISTRY VERY CLEAR FROM THE LORD.

DIFFERENT TYPES OF MINISTRY

"Having then gifts differing according to the grace that is given to us, whether prophecy, let us prophesy according to the proportion of faith; Or ministry, let us wait on our ministering: or he that teacheth, on teaching; Or he that exhorteth, on exhortation: he that giveth, let him do it with simplicity; he that ruleth, with diligence; he that sheweth mercy, with cheerfulness."

- ROM. 12:6-8

91

THE SCRIPTURE REVEALS VARIOUS TYPES OF MINISTRIES. THE FIVE FOLD MINISTRY (APOSTLE, PROPHET, EVANGELIST, PASTOR AND TEACHER) ARE THE LEADERSHIP MINISTRY IN THE CHURCH. THEY TEND TO BE LARGELY FOR MEN: THE PROPENSITY FOR MEN IN LEADERSHIP POSITIONS IS MUCH HIGHER IN THE SCRIPTURE. HOWEVER, OTHER MINISTRY SUCH AS HELPS, GIVING, SINGING, INTERCESSION, CARING AND SUPPORTING ARE LARGELY FOR WOMEN. THE KITCHEN AND MATERNITY HOME ARE NOT THE ONLY PLACE FOR WOMEN MINISTRY.

TODAY, MUCH PROBLEMS HAVE RISEN BECAUSE MANY WOMEN WHO ARE CALLED INTO MINISTRY HAVE DABBLED INTO CHURCH PLANTING AND FOUNDING. LACK OF PROPER UNDERSTANDING OF THE VISION HAVE WRONGLY LED MANY TO START AND LEAD STRUGGLING CHURCHES WITH THE ATTENDANT CHAOS AND CRISIS.

MINISTRY MUST NOT BE CONFUSED WITH THE CHURCH. MINISTRY IS NOT IN COMPETITION WITH THE LOCAL CHURCH. EVERY GOD GIVEN MINISTRY MUST EDIFY, BLESS, HELP AND GROW THE LOCAL CHURCH. THE PRINCIPAL DIFFERENCE BETWEEN MINISTRY AND CHURCH IS THIS: WHILE MINISTRY IS OUTREACH, EVANGELISTIC AND TEACHING ORIENTED WITH NO SUNDAY WORSHIP; CHURCH IS TEACHING, ASSIMILATION, INTEGRATION AND DISCIPLESHIP ORIENTED WITH SUNDAY WORSHIP AND WEEKLY PROGRAMMES. GOD IS RAISING MANY WOMEN FOR MINISTRY AT THIS END TIME.

THE FOLLOWING ARE SOME OF THE MINISTRY AREAS THAT GOD IS USING MANY WOMEN:

A.   MINISTRY TO CHILDREN AND YOUTH (II TIM. 1:5)
B.   COUNSELLING MINISTRY (ACTS 18:26)
C.   MINISTRY OF HOSPITALITY (MATT. 25:36)
D.   DRAMA MINISTRY (I COR. 9:19-23)
E.   MINISTRY TO DRUG ADDICTS (MATT. 28:19-20)
F.   PRISON MINISTRY (MATT. 25:42)
G.   MINISTRY TO OLD PEOPLE (MATT. 25:42)
H.   MINISTRY TO PROSTITUTES AND SINGLE MOTHERS (MATT. 25:43)
I.   MINISTRY TO MARKET WOMEN (ACTS 17:4)
J.   MINISTRY OF INTERCESSION AND WARFARE (ESTHER 4:15-17)
K.   MINISTRY TO BUSINESS WOMEN (ACTS 16:14)
L.   MINISTRY OF HELPS AND SPONSORSHIP (LUKE 8:1-3)
M.   MINISTRY TO PROFESSIONALS
N.   MINISTRY TO FAMILIES AND HOMES
O.   MINISTRY OF SINGING AND WORSHIP (EXOD. 15:20-21)
P.   MINISTRY OF DELIVERANCE AND FREEDOM (OBADIAH 17)
Q.   MINISTRY OF THE PROPHETIC (II KINGS 22:14; LUKE 2:36-37)

FACTS ABOUT MINISTRY

A.   YOUR SUCCESS, PROMOTION, MONEY AND PROSPERITY DEPENDS ON OBEDIENCE TO YOUR MINISTRY.
B.   YOU CANNOT ENJOY GOD'S BLESSING

OUTSIDE YOUR MINISTRY.
C. YOU CANNOT SUCCEED OUTSIDE GOD'S MINISTRY FOR YOU.
D. LOCATING YOUR MINISTRY IS THE KEY TO YOUR LOCATION.
E. YOUR IMPACT IN LIFE DEPENDS ON FAITHFULNESS TO YOUR MINISTRY.
F. WORKING OUTSIDE OF YOUR MINISTRY IS BEING OUT OF GOD'S FAVOUR, BLESSING, PEACE, PROMOTION AND PROTECTION.

MINISTRY MUST'S FOR IMPACT

TO MAKE LASTING AND WORTHWHILE IMPACT THROUGH THE MINISTRY THAT GOD HAS GIVEN TO YOU WOULD DEMAND THAT YOU DO THE FOLLOWING:

A. STRONG RELATIONSHIP WITH THE LORD (MARK 1:35)
B. LISTEN AND OBEY HIS DIRECTION (JOHN 9:14-15)
C. PERSONAL DEVELOPMENT AND GROWTH (II PETER 1:5-11)
D. COURAGE AND BOLDNESS (JOSH. 1:7)
E. PURSUE THE GOAL DILIGENTLY.
F. DON'T GIVE UP TO TEMPORARY FAILURES.
G. DON'T SETTLE FOR AVERAGE, GO FOR

CHAPTER TEN

PITFALLS OF FEMALE MINISTERS TODAY

A CERTAIN WOMAN WAS HIGHLY ANOINTED BY THE LORD TO BE A 'BARRENNESS BULLDOZER'. SHE HAD THIS ANOINTING TO PRAY FRUITFULNESS INTO EVERY BARREN WOMAN. HER MINISTRY WAS GROWING IN LEAPS AND BOUNDS. GOD USED VARIOUS PEOPLE IN WONDERFUL WAYS TO HELP AND PROSPER THE MINISTRY. BUT THE PROBLEM IS THAT THE WOMAN OF GOD RULES OVER HER HUSBAND. SHE MADE HIM ONE OF THE DEACONS IN THE CHURCH AND WOULD PUBLICLY CALL HIM OUT AND LAY HANDS ON HIM, IN THE NAME OF RENEWING THE ANOINTING. GOOD AND SENSITIVE PEOPLE WERE REPULSED AND GRADUALLY BUT SURELY, THE MINISTRY BEGAN TO WITTLE DOWN. TODAY, THE MINISTRY IS A MERE SHADOW OF HER FORMER SELF.

THE MORE I RELATE WITH, TEACH AND MENTOR FEMALE MINISTERS, THE MORE I SEE THE NEED TO ADDRESS GLARING ERRORS THAT ARE PREVALENT AMONG THESE WONDERFUL WOMEN. UNFORTUNATELY, NOBODY IS ADDRESSING THEM AND THEY ARE SPREADING LIKE WILD-FIRE. HOWEVER, THESE PRACTICES ARE PITFALLS THAT HAS RUINED MANY GREAT WOMEN OF GOD. AND IF YOU DON'T ADDRESS THEM SQUARELY IN YOUR LIFE, THEY MIGHT RUIN YOU TOO.

1. WRONG FOUNDATION

LOTS OF FEMALE MINISTERS ARE IN MINISTRY OR DOING MINISTRY INSPITE OF THEIR HUSBANDS. THEY DON'T GET THE APPROVAL OF THEIR HUSBANDS, YET THEY ARE DOING MINISTRY. THEY DISOBEYED THEIR HUSBANDS AND ABANDONED EVERYTHING FOR 'MINISTRY'. WELL, SUCH WOMEN ARE BREAKING THE DIVINE ORDER. YOU CANNOT SUCCEED IN MINISTRY WITHOUT THE APPROVAL AND SUPPORT OF YOUR HUSBAND. HE IS YOUR HEAD AND WHEN YOU NEGLECT YOUR HEAD, YOU ARE HEADED FOR DISASTER.

You cannot succeed in ministry without the approval and support of your husband.

WHEN YOU SENSED THE CALL OF GOD IN YOUR LIFE TO A PARTICULAR AREA OF MINISTRY, YOU MUST ALSO PRAY EARNESTLY THAT GOD WILL GO AND CONVINCE YOUR HUSBAND, SO THAT HE CAN RELEASE YOU FOR THE MINISTRY. IF NOT, THE CALL

WILL NOT REALLY WORK. NO MATTER HOW 'STUBBORN' OR 'DIFFICULT' A MAN MAY PROVE TO BE, YOUR PRAYERS, LOVE, GOOD MANNERS AND RESPECT FOR HIM WILL WIN HIM OVER TO YOUR SIDE.

I HAVE SEEN MANY WOMEN NEGLECTING THEIR HUSBANDS AND SPENDING THEIR LIFE DOING MINISTRY IN DISOBEDIENCE, THE MORE REASON THEIR WORK IS UNFRUITFUL. IF YOU BUILD YOUR MINISTRY IN DISOBEDIENCE AND LACK OF RESPECT FOR YOUR HUSBAND, THEN THAT IS A WRONG FOUNDATION THAT WILL COLLAPSE SOONER OR LATER, IRRESPECTIVE OF FINE STRUCTURE YOU BUILD ON IT. THIS IS A GREAT PITFALL THAT MANY FEMALE MINISTERS HAVE FALLEN INTO. YOU MUST AVOID IT IN YOUR LIFE.

2. DOMINATING YOUR HUSBAND

A CERTAIN FEMALE MINISTER WAS CALLED TO THE MINISTRY. THE HUSBAND SUPPORTED HER AND HELPED HER FINANCIALLY. HE EVEN BOUGHT A PIECE OF LAND FOR THE WIFE TO ERECT HER CHURCH BUILDING. AFTER THE BUILDING WAS ERECTED AND THE CHURCH WAS GROWING, THE LADY STARTED DOMINATING THE HUSBAND. SHE OPERATED WITH THE ATTITUDE THAT SHE IS A GENERAL OVERSEER IN THE CHURCH AND EVERYBODY RESPECTED HER. SHE EXPECTED AND DEMANDED FOR THE SAME RESPECT AT HOME. SHE WANTED THE HUSBAND TO BE AT HER BECK AND CALL, DOING ALL THE HOUSE CHORES, RUNNING ERRANDS FOR HER AND ANSWERS WITH OBEISANCE WHENEVER SHE CALLS HIM.

WELL, THIS WENT ON FOR SOMETIME UNTIL THE HUSBAND REGAINED HIS MANLINESS. HE OBJECTED STRONGLY TO HER DOMINANCE AND A FIGHT ENSUED. SHE PACKED OUT AND MOVED TO THE CHURCH, AND THE HUSBAND DECIDED TO RECLAIM THE PIECE OF LAND HE BOUGHT FOR THE CHURCH. THIS LED TO DIVORCE AND COURT CASES.

ALL THESE SCENARIOS CAME ABOUT BECAUSE THE FEMALE MINISTER REFUSED TO SEPARATE BETWEEN HER ROLE AS A WIFE AND AS A GOSPEL MINISTER. FEMALE MINISTERS NEED TO REALIZE THAT INSPITE OF THEIR CALLING INTO THE MINISTRY. THEY ARE STILL A WIVES TO MEN AND MOTHERS TO THE CHILDREN. IN THE CHURCH, YOU MIGHT BE THE OVERALL LEADER THAT EVERYBODY RESPECTS AND OBEYS, BUT AT HOME, YOU ARE A WIFE AND YOU MUST BE ALIVE TO YOUR RESPONSIBILITIES, ELSE, YOU WILL RUIN YOURSELF AND THE WORK, JUST LIKE THE WOMAN IN THE STORY ABOVE.

3. FIGHTING THE HUSBAND OVER CHURCH

A MINISTERIAL COUPLE CAME TO ME FOR COUNSELING. THE WIFE WAS THE ONE THAT FIRST RECEIVED THE CALL AND STARTED THE CHURCH. THE HUSBAND LATER RECEIVED THE CALL AND JOINED HER. THEY WERE BOTH MINISTERS OVER THE CHURCH. BUT THE WIFE USED THE PULPIT TO FIGHT THE HUSBAND BECAUSE SHE FELT THE HUSBAND WAS TRYING TO TAKE THE MINISTRY AWAY FROM HER. IT GOT TO A STAGE THAT THE CHURCH BECAME

98

POLARIZED, WITH ONE GROUP SUPPORTING THE WIFE AND ANOTHER GROUP SUPPORTING THE HUSBAND. TRY AS MUCH AS I COULD, I WAS UNABLE TO RECONCILE THEM AND THE CHURCH HAS DRASTICALLY GONE DOWN NUMERICALLY AS A RESULT OF THE INFIGHTING BETWEEN THE HUSBAND AND WIFE. IT HAS EVEN AFFECTED THEIR HOME ADVERSELY BECAUSE THE WIFE WOULD NO LONGER GIVE HER BODY TO THE HUSBAND AND HE TOO WENT OUT TO SATISFY HIMSELF. WHAT A SHAME! HOWEVER, THIS PITFALL IS WHAT MANY FEMALE MINISTERS HAVE FALLEN INTO TODAY AND THEIR HOMES AND MINISTRY ARE BEING NEGATIVELY AFFECTED.

THERE SHOULD BE NO REASON THAT WOULD MAKE A MINISTERIAL COUPLE TO FIGHT EACH OTHER OVER THE CHURCH. IT IS ONLY CARNALITY, IMMATURITY AND DEMONIC INFLUENCE THAT BREED SUCH. WIVES SHOULD EMPLOY HUMILITY, PRAYERS AND MATURED ATTITUDES TO HANDLE SUCH ISSUES UNTIL THE LORD WILL BRING SETTLEMENT IN HIS OWN PECULIAR WAYS.

4. RUNNING CHURCH INSTEAD OF MINISTRY

AS I HAVE NOTED IN THE PREVIOUS CHAPTER, THE PROPENDURANCE IN THE SCRIPTURE AND SECULAR HISTORY IS THAT GOD CALLS MORE MEN TO CHURCH LEADERSHIP THAN WOMEN. MORE MEN ARE CALLED TO BE PASTORS, APOSTLES, TEACHERS AND EVANGELISTS THAN WOMEN. THOUGH THESE FIVE-FOLD CHURCH LEADERSHIP GIFTS ARE NOT THE EXCLUSIVE RIGHT OF MEN, YET THE SCALE TILTS

MORE TOWARDS MEN THAN WOMEN. MOST WOMEN ARE THEREFORE CALLED TO MINISTRIES THAT WILL BLESS THE BODY OF CHRIST AND BUILD HIS KINGDOM. MINISTRIES TO CHILDREN, YOUTH, PROSTITUTES, SINGLE MOTHERS, COUNSELLING AND MANY OTHERS ARE MUCH MORE FOR WOMEN THAN MEN.

UNFORTUNATELY, MOST FEMALE MINISTERS HAVE NOT TAKEN TIME TO DISCERN THEIR MINISTRIES, BUT HAVE JUMPED INTO THE DELICATE ISSUE OF CHURCH PLANTING. THEY HAVE STARTED CHURCHES INSTEAD OF RUNNING MINISTRIES AND THE RESULTS HAVE BEEN STAGNATION, CRISIS AND STUNTED GROWTH.

Any ministry you purport to be doing, without your home is a hogwash.

WHEN YOU HAVE THE MINISTRY OF SINGING AND WORSHIP, DON'T TURN IT INTO CHURCH. THOSE FEMALE MINISTERS WHO DID, ARE REGRETTING AND BITING THEIR FINGERS. WHEN YOU ARE GIVEN COUNSELING, SINGLES, INTERCESSORY AND GIVING GIFTS, RUN THEM AS MINISTRY WITH OFFICE, STAFF AND OUTREACHES. DON'T EVER TURN THEM TO CHURCH BECAUSE THE GRACE TO RUN A MINISTRY IS QUITE DIFFERENT FROM THE ONE TO LEAD A CHURCH. AND WHEN YOU FUNCTION WHERE GOD HAS NOT GIVEN YOU THE GRACE, YOU WILL STRUGGLE A LOT AND ULTIMATELY FAIL.

5. **MAKING THE HUSBAND THE**

GENERAL OVERSEER, THOUGH HE IS NOT CALLED

I HAVE COME ACROSS SEVERAL FEMALE MINISTERS WHO HAVE MADE THIS GRAVE MISTAKE. IN PSEUDO-HUMILITY, THEY MADE THEIR HUSBANDS THE TOPMOST LEADER OF THEIR CHURCHES, EVEN THOUGH GOD HAS NOT CALLED THE HUSBAND. IN MOST CASES, THE HUSBAND BECOMES THE ARCHITECT OF THE DOWNFALL OF THE CHURCH. WHEN A MAN IS OPERATING AT THE POSITION AND ROLE HE HAS NO ANOINTING AND GRACE FOR, THEN HE WILL MESS UP BIGTIME. IN ONE OF SUCH CASES, THE HUSBAND MESSED UP WITH GIRLS IN THE CHURCH UNTIL THE BUBBLE BURSTED. THE MINISTRY ALMOST WENT UNDER BECAUSE OF IT.

WHEN YOU ARE CALLED TO PLANT AND LEAD A CHURCH AS A FEMALE MINISTER, YOU MUST NEVER PLACE YOUR HUSBAND IN THE POSITION GOD HAS NOT ORDAINED AND QUALIFIED HIM FOR. DON'T BE TOO HUMBLE TO LEAD WHAT GOD HAS CALLED YOU TO DO. THE BEST YOU CAN DO IS TO ALLOW HIM TO BE A DEACON OR AN ELDER IN THE CHURCH. AT HOME, HE IS THE UNDISPUTABLE LEADER, BUT IN CHURCH, YOU MUST LEAD THE WORK AND GIVE HIM HIS RESPECT AS A GOOD SUPPORTER OF THE VISION. MAKING HIM THE GENERAL OVERSEER WILL OPEN HIM UP TO MANY ATTACKS, WHICH WILL HAVE NEGATIVE RESULTS ON THE CHURCH.

6. COPYING POPULAR FEMALE MINISTERS

I HAVE WATCHED WITH DISMAY AS YOUNG FEMALE MINISTERS COPY HOOK, LINE AND SINKER, THE BAD EXAMPLES OF POPULAR FEMALE MINISTERS. ONE OF SUCH BAD EXAMPLE BEING COPIED IS LIFTING THE MINISTRY MORE THAN THE FAMILY. FEMALE MINISTERS WHO OPERATE WITH THIS MINDSET NEGLECT THEIR HUSBAND AND CHILDREN IN THE NAME OF MINISTRY. SOME OF THEM EVEN DIVORCED THEIR HUSBANDS, REMARRIED AND DIVORCED AGAIN, YET THEY ARE STILL DOING 'MINISTRY'. PAULA WHITE, JUANITA BUNYAN ARE PRIME EXAMPLES IN THIS MESS. BACK HOME IN NIGERIA, IT IS COMMON KNOWLEDGE THAT CHILDREN OF FEMALE MINISTERS DRESS LIKE PROSTITUTES, SLEEP WITH BOYFRIENDS HERE AND THERE, AND ARE FAR AWAY FROM GOD IN THEIR CHOICES AND LIFESTYLES, ALL BECAUSE THEIR MOTHERS ARE 'DEEPLY' INVOLVED IN THE MINISTRY AND THEREFORE HAVE NO TIME FOR THEM. SHE WOULD LEAVE HOME IN THE MORNING AFTER GIVING INSTRUCTIONS AND RETURN LATE AT NIGHT TO PASS JUDGMENT, NEVER KNOWING WHAT THE CHILDREN DID DURING THE DAY.

FURTHERMORE, THESE SET OF FEMALE MINISTERS, HATE MEN IN THEIR LIVES AND SEE HUSBANDS AS HINDRANCES TO THEIR LIVES AND 'MINISTRY'. TO THEM, MINISTRY IS MUCH MORE IMPORTANT THAN HUSBAND AND CHILDREN. WHAT AN ERROR! ANY MINISTRY YOU PURPORT TO BE DOING, WITHOUT YOUR HOME IS A HOGWASH. NEGLECTING YOUR HOME IN THE NAME OF MINISTRY IS INCOMPATIBLE WITH THE SCRIPTURE. YOUR NUMBER ONE MINISTRY MUST BE YOUR HUSBAND AND CHILDREN. IF YOU

FAIL AT HOME, YOU HAVE FAILED TOTALLY. EVERY MINISTRY YOU DO MUST START AND END AT HOME. AND IF IT DOESN'T WORK AT HOME, IT'S POINTLESS EXPORTING IT ABROAD.

7. EGO LEADERSHIP

BOASTING, EGO TRIP AND THROWING YOUR WEIGHT AROUND IS A COMMON PITFALL THAT HAS SWALLOWED UP MANY FEMALE MINISTERS. DOMINATING MEN THAT SERVE UNDER YOU AND BOASTING OF WHAT YOU HAVE ACHIEVED WILL NOT TAKE YOU ANYWHERE BUT DOWN. SOME FEMALE MINISTERS HAVE STRONG ISSUES WITH EGO TRIP. THEY DEMAND FOR FIRST CLASS TICKETS, FIVE STAR HOTELS, SIREN DRIVEN CONVOYS AND SPECIALIZED FOODS AND PROTOCOLS IN THE NAME OF BRANDING AND PUTTING VALUE ON THEMSELVES. THEY BECOME HIGH MAINTENANCE FOR UNFORTUNATE CHURCHES THAT INVITE THEM.

THEY ARE TOUCHY, IRRITATING AND MANNERLESS. THEY BEHAVE AS IF THEY ARE DOING YOU A FAVOUR FOR HONOURING YOUR INVITATION. THEY ABUSE, CASTIGATE AND ARE TEMPERAMENTAL TO THEIR ASSOCIATES. THEY DON'T DELEGATE AS NOBODY CAN DO IT LIKE THEM AND EVERYTHING REVOLVES AROUND THEM. SUCH EGOISTIC BEHAVIOURS ALWAYS RUIN MINISTERS AND MINISTRIES. THOUGH SOME OF THEM WILL TRY TO DEFEND THEMSELVES WITH SOME PLAUSIBLE REASONS, YET, TRUTH BE TOLD, EGO AND PRIDE ARE INEXCUSABLE IN A GOSPEL MINISTER, NO MATTER HOW ANOINTED.

8. MESSING AROUND WITH MEN

MANY OF THE DIVORCED, SEPARATED AND SINGLE FEMALE MINISTERS ARE INTO IMMORALITIES AND SEXUAL PERVERSION. SOME OF THEM FLIRT AROUND WITH MEN AFTER MINISTRATIONS OR FROLICK WITH MALE PASTORS. SOME DIVORCED THEIR HUSBANDS AND SEDUCED MEN TO MARRY THEM IN THE CHURCH TO SATISFY THEIR HIGH SEXUAL PASSIONS. THERE ARE STORIES OF LADY BISHOPS WHO CHANGE MEN AT WILL AND SLEEP WITH ANY MAN THAT CATCHES THEIR FANCY, AND HAVE RUINED ONCE GREAT MINISTRIES.

JESUS EVEN MENTIONED A PROPHETESS IN HIS SEVEN LETTERS TO THE CHURCHES, WHO HAS A PENCHANT FOR SEDUCING MEN TO SLEEP WITH HER IN THE CHURCH (REV. 2:20). SOME FEMALE MINISTERS ARE STILL OPERATING WITH THAT SPIRIT TODAY. IT WAS THE LORD THAT SAVED ME FROM ONE OF THEM. SHE TRIED TO SEDUCE ME WHEN SHE INVITED ME TO COME AND TRAIN HER UNDER-LEADERS. ONE TIME, SHE EVEN GAVE ME A MALE PANT AS GIFT! I HAD TO RUN AWAY FROM HER AND FORGET THE MONIES OF MY BOOKS WITH HER, SINCE SHE PROMISED NOT TO PAY UNLESS I COME TO HER HOUSE TO PICK THE MONEY IN THE AFTERNOON WHEN NOBODY WILL BE AROUND.

I have come to realize that choosing a wrong mentor is one of the pitfalls that female ministers fall into.

ANOTHER ONE GAVE ME

BEDSPREAD TWICE AS GIFT AND SAID SHE WANTED ME TO ALWAYS REMEMBER HER WHEN I'M SLEEPING ON THE BED WITH MY WIFE! CAN YOU BEAT THAT? I HAD TO BURN THE FIRST ONE AND GAVE THE SECOND ONE AWAY! SUCH IMMORAL WOMEN ARE AROUND IN THE MINISTRY TODAY AND ARE RUINING THE LIFE OF UNSUSPECTING MEN. AS JESUS PRONOUNCED JUDGMENT ON PROPHETESS JEZEBEL, SO ALSO SUCH WOMEN WILL BE SEVERELY JUDGED IF THEY FAIL TO REPENT OF THEIR EVIL DEEDS.

9.   DENYING THE HUSBAND SEX

THE HUSBAND OF A FEMALE MINISTER RAN TO MY OFFICE THE OTHER DAY, COMPLAINING BITTERLY THAT HIS WIFE WAS PUNISHING HIM WITH SEX. I PACIFIED HIM AND PUT A CALL THROUGH TO THE WIFE. SHE CAME AND ALL HER EXCUSES WERE WHAT THE AVERAGE FEMALE MINISTERS GIVE, 'MY HUSBAND DEMANDS FOR TOO MUCH SEX', 'SEX REDUCES THE ANOINTING'; 'I HAVE TO PREPARE FOR MINISTRATIONS AND KEEP MYSELF PRIME FOR MY MINISTRY'. WELL, I TOLD HER POINT BLANK THAT UNLESS SHE IS SICK OR IN HER MONTHLY CYCLES, SHE MUST NEVER DENY HER HUSBAND SEX AGAIN. SHE AGREED AFTER MUCH PERSUASION AND HER HOME HAS BECOME BETTER SINCE THEN.

FEMALE MINISTERS HAVE TURNED IT TO A ROUTINE

LADY EVANGELISTS AND PROPHETESSES

THE SCRIPTURE IS CLEAR THAT GOD DID NOT ONLY POUR OUT HIS SPIRIT UPON MEN ALONE, BUT ALSO ON WOMEN.

> *"And it shall come to pass in the last days, saith God, I will pour out of my Spirit upon all flesh: and your sons and your daughters shall prophesy, and your young men shall see visions, and your old men shall dream dreams: And on my servants and on my handmaidens I will pour out in those days of my Spirit; and they shall prophesy"*

ACTS 2:17-18.

GOD HAS BEEN AND IS STILL USING LOTS OF

WOMEN IN HIS VINEYARD. SOMETIMES, THESE WOMEN, EITHER YOUNG OR OLD, HIGH OR LOW, EDUCATED OR UNEDUCATED, FUNCTION AS EVANGELISTS OR PROPHETESSES. THEY BRING THE GOOD NEWS OF THE GOSPEL TO ALL AND SUNDRY AND ALSO FUNCTION AS THE MOUTHPIECE OF GOD IN UTTERING PROPHETIC WORDS INTO LIVES AND SITUATIONS. SOME OF THESE WOMEN HAVE GONE AHEAD TO START PROPHETIC CHURCHES, MINISTRIES AND EVANGELISTIC OUTREACHES. BUT LOTS OF UNWHOLESOME PRACTICES DEMAND THAT WE TAKE A GOOD LOOK AT THESE WOMEN VESSELS AGAIN.

A. BIBLICAL AND CONTEMPORARY EXAMPLES:

VARIOUS EXAMPLES ABOUND IN THE SCRIPTURES AND OUR CONTEMPORARY WORLD OF WOMEN GOD USED MIGHTILY IN HIS VINEYARD TO PROPAGATE THE GOSPEL AND EXPAND THE FRONTIERS OF HIS KINGDOM. AMONG THEM ARE; MIRIAM WHO WAS A PROPHETESS AND A WORSHIP LEADER (EXOD. 15:20), DEBORAH WAS A NATIONAL LEADER AND PROPHETESS (JUDGES 4:4), HULDAH WAS A NATIONAL PROPHETESS (2 KINGS 22:14), NOADIAH WAS A RECOGNIZED PROPHETESS (NEH. 6:14), ANNA WAS A PROPHETESS (LUKE 2:36), THE DAUGHTERS OF PHILIP (ACTS 21:9), AND THE WOMAN EVANGELIST IN JOHN CHAPTER 4 VERSE 29.

THESE WOMEN PROPHETESSES WERE MIGHTILY USED BY THE LORD TO BRING PERSONAL AND NATIONAL HEALING, HARMONY AND RESTORATION TO THE NATION OF ISRAEL. THEY FUNCTIONED AS INTERCESSORS, PRAYER WARRIORS AND BATTLE

108

LEADERS TO FREE THEIR NATION AND PEOPLE FROM BONDAGE AND BRING THE PROMISE OF GOD INTO REALITY.

IN CONTEMPORARY HISTORY, WE HAVE THE LIKES OF; KATHERINE KHULMAN, JASHIL CHO, MADAME GUYON AND ELIZABETH DABNEY.

B. MARKS OF FALSE OR PHONEY PROPHETESSES AND LADY EVANGELISTS

A LADY EVANGELIST WAS INVITED TO MINISTER IN A CHURCH. WHILE MINISTERING, SHE NOTICED A WELL-DRESSED MAN. SHE CALLED THE MAN OUT AND TOLD HIM SHE HAD A SPECIAL MESSAGE FOR HIM. SHE TOLD THE MAN THAT HIS WIFE WAS A WITCH AND THAT THE MAN WOULD KNOW IN HIS DREAM. SHE MANIPULATED THE MAN'S DREAM BY PUTTING ON THE IMAGE OF THE WIFE AND PURSUED HIM IN THE DREAM. THE MAN SENT THE WIFE PACKING AND EVENTUALLY MARRIED THE LADY EVANGELIST.

"Notwithstanding I have a few things against thee, because thou sufferest that woman Jezebel, which calleth herself a prophetess, to teach and to seduce my servants to commit fornication, and to eat things sacrificed unto idols. And I gave her space to repent of her fornication; and she repented not. Behold, I will cast her into a bed, and them that commit adultery with her into great tribulation, except they repent of their deeds. And I will kill her children with death; and all the churches shall know that I am he which searcheth the reins and hearts: and I will give unto every one of you according to your

109

works."-

- REV. 2:20-23

TODAY, WE HAVE MANY WOMEN WHO CLAIM TO BE PROPHETESSES AND EVANGELISTS. WHILE MANY OF THEM ARE CHURCH FOUNDERS, OTHERS SERVE AS EVANGELISTS, SINGERS AND WORSHIP LEADERS, ASSISTING MINISTERS AND WORKERS IN THE VINEYARD OF THE LORD. HOWEVER, A HIGHER PERCENTAGE ARE DISPLAYING THE TRAITS OF PHONEY MINISTERS. THEY BEHAVE LIKE ATALIAH AND JEZEBEL (2 KINGS 11:1; I KINGS 2:25; 2 KINGS 9:30). ONE SO CALLED PROPHETESS WAS ONCE ATTRACTING CROWD TO HER CHURCH WITH WITCHCRAFT. SHE WAS FOND OF USING FAKE AND PHONY PROPHECIES TO CONTROL PEOPLE UNTIL HER SECRET WAS EXPOSED BY A YOUNG GIRL WHO CONFESSED THAT THEY BOTH BELONGED TO A WITCHCRAFT COVEN.

ANOTHER ONE SEDUCED THREE YOUNG MEN IN HER CHURCH TO BE SLEEPING WITH HER UNTIL HER HUSBAND CAUGHT HER ON THEIR MATRIMONIAL BED.

THE FOLLOWING ARE SOME OF THEIR TRAITS AND IDENTIFICATION MARKS:
* OPERATING WITH WITCHCRAFT SPIRIT IN PROPHECY.
* FULL OF STRIFE, QUARREL AND ANIMOSITY.

If you are working with a male pastor, be open, transparent, careful and dignified.

* LUSFUL, SEDUCTIVE, IMMORAL AND SEXUAL PERVASION.
* FAILURE TO TAKE CARE OF HOME, HUSBAND AND CHILDREN.
* PURSUING VAIN, WORLDLY, CARNAL AND EPHEMERAL THINGS.
* USING PROPHECY TO HOODWINK, MANIPULATE AND CAUSE DIVISION.
* BIBLICAL ILLITERACY AND SPIRITUAL SHALLOWNESS.
* STUBBORNNESS, PRIDE, DISOBEDIENCE AND SELF-WILLED.
* BICKERING, RUMOR-MONGERING, TALE BEARING, ENVY AND JEALOUSY.
* DIVORCING HUSBANDS IN THE NAME OF MINISTRY AND ELOPING WITH OTHER MEN.
* FULL OF BITTERNESS, UNFORGIVING SPIRIT AND CRITICAL SPIRIT.

UNFORTUNATELY, TOO MANY LADY EVANGELISTS AND PROPHETESSES ARE FOUND WITH ALL THESE CHARACTERISTICS IN THEIR LIVES. THE MORE REASON THE NAME OF CHRIST IS BEING SPOKEN EVIL OF BY UNBELIEVERS TODAY. WOMEN THAT REALLY WANT TO PLEASE THE LORD AND BE TRULY USED BY HIM MUST PURGE THESE EVIL TRAITS OUT OF THEIR LIVES.

IF YOU ARE WORKING WITH A MALE PASTOR, BE OPEN, TRANSPARENT, CAREFUL AND DIGNIFIED. BE THE BEST FRIEND OF HIS WIFE AND BE OPEN WITH HER. DON'T GO TOO CLOSE WITH HIM, LET IT BE STRICTLY MINISTRY.

C.   MARKS OF TRULY CAPABLE LADY

111

EVANGELISTS AND PROPHETESSES

TODAY, THE CHURCH NEEDS MUCH MORE TRULY CAPABLE WOMEN THAT WILL FUNCTION AS PROPHETESSES AND EVANGELISTS TO THE NATIONS. THE CHURCH, WORLD, MEN AND THE SOCIETY NEED SUCH WOMEN. HOWEVER, THEY MUST BE WOMEN THAT ARE SPIRITUALLY, PHYSICALLY, MENTALLY, ECONOMICALLY AND FINANCIALLY CAPABLE LIKE ABIGAIL IN THE SCRIPTURE.

A TRULY CAPABLE WOMAN MINISTER MUST POSSESS THE FOLLOWING CHARACTERISTICS;

I. TRUE KNOWLEDGE AND RELATIONSHIP WITH LORD (LUKE 7:37-38).
II. A DEVOUT WIFE AND MOTHER TO HER CHILDREN AND ALL (I KINGS 22:14)
III. A WOMAN OF GODLY SOBRIETY, CHARACTER AND KIND SPIRIT (ACTS 9:36).
IV. STRONG FAITH IN THE LORD AND NOT GIVEN

THE MATURED WOMAN MINISTER TODAY

MORE AND MORE, GOD IS RAISING MANY WOMEN UP TO BE USED MIGHTILY AT THIS END TIME. THE SPIRIT IS BEING POURED OUT UPON DAUGHTERS AND HANDMAIDENS OF THE LORD FOR THE END TIME RIPENED HARVEST.

"And it shall come to pass in the last days, saith God, I will pour out of my Spirit upon all flesh: and your sons and your daughters shall prophesy, and your young men shall see visions, and your old men shall dream dreams: And on my servants and on my handmaidens I will pour out in those days of my Spirit; and they shall prophesy:"

ACTS 2:17-18.

113

MANY CHURCHES ARE GRADUALLY ACCEPTING WOMEN IN MINISTRY AND EVEN AS PASTORS OF CHURCHES. AND MANY ARE DOING EXPLOITS FOR THE LORD. HOWEVER, THERE ARE LOTS OF ISSUES THAT NEED TO BE ADDRESSED IF MUCH MORE IMPACT IS GOING TO BE MADE BY WOMEN MINISTERS.

THE PLACE OF WOMEN MINISTERS

THE CALLING OF GOD IS NOT ONLY ON MEN, BUT ALSO ON WOMEN. IN BIBLE TIMES, GOD CALLED SELECTED WOMEN TO DO GREAT WORKS FOR HIM. FOR EXAMPLE; MIRIAM (EXOD. 2:7; 15:20-21), DEBORAH (JUDGES 4:4-5), HULDAH (II KINGS 22:14), ANNA (LUKE 2:36-37), PHILIP'S FOUR DAUGHTERS (ACTS 21:8-9), PRISCILLA (ACTS 18:24-28), PHOEBE (ROMANS 16:1-2) AND SYNTYCHE (PHIL. 4:3).

The Lord expects every female minister to be strong in faith and a good example of who a minister of God should be.

THESE WOMEN HELD LEADERSHIP AND MINISTERIAL POSITIONS IN THE SCRIPTURE. GOD USED MANY OF THEM WITH AND ALONGSIDE THEIR HUSBANDS. AND SOME OF THEM MINISTERED ALONE, EITHER AS WIDOWS OR UNMARRIED. IN WHATEVER STATE, GOD HAS NO INHIBITION IN RAISING, CALLING, ANOINTING AND USING WOMEN MIGHTILY FOR HIS KINGDOM.

GOD'S EXPECTATION OF A FEMALE

MINISTER

*"I commend unto you Phoebe our sister, which is
a servant of the church which is at Cenchrea:
That ye receive her in the Lord, as becometh
saints, and that ye assist her in whatsoever
business she hath need of you: for she hath been
a succourer of many, and of myself also."*
                                        - ROMANS 16:1-2

EVERY CALLED AND COMMISSIONED FEMALE
MINISTER IS EXPECTED BY GOD TO IMBIBE THE
FOLLOWING QUALITIES:
*   GENUINE SALVATION AND DEEP RELATIONSHIP
WITH GOD.
*   MATURED BEHAVIOUR AND GODLY
        CHARACTERS.
*   FOCUS ON DISTINCT MINISTRY AND CALLING.
*   A GODLY MOTHER, WIFE AND MINISTER.
*   RESPECTABLE, HONOURABLE AND NOBLE
        COMPORTMENT.
*   TRUTHFUL, LOYAL, SINCERE AND GENUINE IN
        ALL THINGS.
*   GROWING, IMPROVING, RELEVANT AND UP-TO-
        DATE.
*   KEEP A GOOD HOME AND EXAMPLE OF
        GODLINESS.
*   FRUITS OF THE SPIRIT AND GODLY VALUES.
*   FERVENT IN THE SPIRIT AND DEVOTION TO
        KINGDOM GROWTH.

THE LORD EXPECTS EVERY FEMALE MINISTER TO BE STRONG IN FAITH AND A GOOD EXAMPLE OF WHO A MINISTER OF GOD SHOULD BE. INSPITE OF PERSONAL CHALLENGES, EVERY FEMALE MINISTER MUST LIVE UP TO GOD'S EXPECTATION.

KINDS OF FEMALE MINISTERS TODAY

AS MORE AND MORE FEMALE MINISTERS ANSWER THE CALL AND COME INTO THE MINISTRY, WE BEGIN TO NOTICE MANY FEATURES IN THEM. HERE ARE SOME KINDS THAT WE HAVE DISCOVERED:

1. THE DIVA:

THIS WOMAN IS A STAR AND MINISTRY IS ALL ABOUT HER. SURELY, SHE STARTED OUT WITH GENUINE PASSION FOR GOD, BUT TODAY, HER MESSAGE IS NOT DEFINED BY HER SECRET PRAYER LIFE BUT BY WHAT PEOPLE SEE ON STAGE. GREED AND PRIDE HAVE DECEPTIVELY LURED HER INTO COMPROMISE. SHE HOLDS PEOPLE TO RANSOME AND DEMANDS FOR FIRST CLASS TREATMENT EVERYWHERE SHE GOES. YES, SHE CAN MOVE A CROWD BUT SHE IS OF 'HIGH MAINTENANCE'.

2. THE CONTROL FREAK:

THIS WOMAN DOES NOT KNOW HOW TO DELEGATE. SHE IS NOT A TEAM PLAYER. SHE BELIEVES SHE KNOWS ALL THE ANSWERS, AND THEREFORE SHE MUST SIGN

OFF ON ALL DECISIONS, NO MATTER HOW PETTY. PEOPLE LINE UP OUTSIDE HER DOOR NIGHT AND DAY TO GET HER APPROVAL AND SHE VENTS HER ANGER ON ANYONE THAT DOESN'T RESPECT HER DECISION. SHE IS ALL IN ALL AND HAVE NO MENTOR. HER MEMBERS USUALLY GO AWAY AND HER STAFF RESIGNS ON REGULAR BASIS BECAUSE OF HER HASH STYLE AND ABUSIVE WORDS.

3.   THE FLIRT

SHE DRESSES IN A REVEALING MANNER, EVERY CURVE AND CREVICE ON HER BODY IS VISIBLE TO THE OGLING EYES OF MEN IN THE CONGREGATION. SHE IS FASHION CONSCIOUS. SHE KNOWS NO SEXUAL BOUNDRIES. SHE HANGS AROUND WITH MEN ALONE IN THE CHURCH OFFICE. SHE SEPARATES WITH HER HUSBAND AND MOVE IN WITH ANOTHER MAN A MONTH LATER. SHE USES SEXUALLY CHARGED LANGUAGE AND VEILED VULGARITY IN HER SERMONS. HER BEHAVIOURS DRAW MORE ATTENTION TO HER THAN TO THE LORD. HER CONTROVERSIAL LIFESTYLE REPELS PEOPLE FROM COMING TO THE LORD AND THE CHURCH.

4.   THE FLAKE

SHE HAD A LEGITIMATE EXPERIENCE WITH GOD, BUT BECAUSE OF PRIDE SHE BEGINS TO BELIEVE THAT HER GIFT IS UNIQUE. SHE IS ALWAYS IN SUPER-SPIRITUAL

THE MATURED PASTOR'S WIFE & FEMALE MINISTER

MODE AND RARELY ENJOYS THE NORMAL ROUTINES OF LIFE. SHE BELIEVES THAT HER PROPHECIES, GIFTS AND REVELATIONS ARE SUPERIOR TO THAT OF ANYBODY. SHE FALLS INTO ERROR BECAUSE SHE IS NOT ACCOUNTABLE TO ANYONE AND SHE HAS THEREBY WOUND AND HURT MANY LIVES.

5. THE FEMINIST:

SHE IS BITTER AND VENGEFUL AGAINST MEN BECAUSE OF HER PAST EXPERIENCES. SHE BELIEVES THAT WOMEN ARE SUPERIOR TO MEN AND HAVE A MAN-HATING ATTITUDE. SHE HAS NOT FORGIVEN THE MEN WHO HURT HER IN THE PAST, AND SHE INTENDS TO PUNISH THOSE MEN WHO GET IN HER WAY TODAY. HER MESSAGES EXHUDE HATRED TOWARDS MEN AND SURROUNDS HERSELF ONLY WITH WOMEN AND REFUSES TO PUT MEN IN CERTAIN POSITIONS.

6. THE VICTIM:

SHE HAS LOTS OF UNFORTUNATE STORIES TO TELL. EVERYONE IS AGAINST HER. SHE IS SUSPICIOUS OF HER OWN CONGREGATION. OTHER CHURCHES, SHE SAYS, ARE MALIGNING HER. THE DEVIL, SHE INSISTS, HAS TARGETED HER MINISTRY FOR DESTRUCTION. EVERY TRIAL THAT COMES HER WAY CONFIRMS THAT SHE IS THE FOCUS OF DEMONIC CONSPIRACY. SHE USUALLY TELLS SAD STORIES TO ELICIT SYMPATHY.

FURTHERMORE, FEMALE MINISTERS HAVE USED THEIR MANNERLESS AND NEGATIVE ATTITUDES APPROACH TO BRING DEVALUATION TO WOMEN MINISTRY. LOTS OF CHURCH LEADERS ARE WARY OF FEMALE

THE SINGLE WOMAN MINISTER

I T'S AN UNDENIABLE FACT THAT MANY SINGLE WOMEN ARE MINISTERS AND ARE IN MINISTRY TODAY. IT STARTED SLOWLY AND LARGELY UNNOTICED, BUT HAS GROWN INTO A MAJOR FORCE TODAY. MANY MODERN CHURCHES AND DENOMINATIONS HAVE GROWING NUMBER OF SINGLE WOMEN AND SINGLE PARENTS AS THEIR LEADING OR ASSISTING MINISTERS TODAY. EVEN THOUGH MANY OF THESE WONDERFUL WOMEN HAVE DONE VERY WELL, YET THERE ARE CHALLENGES ASSOCIATED WITH THESE GROUP OF MINISTERS THAT NEED TO BE URGENTLY ADDRESSED.

"Now there was at Joppa a certain disciple named Tabitha, which by interpretation is called Dorcas: this

119

woman was full of good works and almsdeeds which she did."

– ACTS 9:36

"And there was one Anna, a prophetess, the daughter of Phanuel, of the tribe of Aser: she was of a great age, and had lived with an husband seven years from her virginity; And she was a widow of about fourscore and four years, which departed not from the temple, but served God with fastings and prayers night and day. And she coming in that instant gave thanks likewise unto the Lord, and spake of him to all them that looked for redemption in Jerusalem. "

- LUKE 2:36-38

DORCAS WAS AN EXAMPLE OF A SINGLE WOMAN MINISTER. THERE WAS NO RECORD OF HER HUSBAND OR MARRIAGE. SHE WAS HOWEVER A GODLY WOMAN, FULL OF GOOD DEEDS AND A POSITIVE TESTIMONIES TO HER COMMUNITY. ANNA WAS ALSO ANOTHER EXAMPLE OF A SINGLE WOMAN MINISTER WHO SERVED GOD FAITHFULLY TILL THE END.

SINGLENESS IN WOMEN CAN COME IN ANY OF THESE WAYS:
* A CALL TO CELIBACY AND SINGLENESS.
* A DETERMINATION TO REMAIN UNMARRIED.
* EARLY DEATH OF THE HUSBAND.
* LATE MARRIAGE DUE TO SPIRITUAL PROBLEMS.
* SEPARATION AND DIVORCE FOR OBVIOUS REASONS.
* LIVING SEPARATELY FROM THE HUSBAND.

AS A RESULT OF THESE POINTS, LOTS OF SINGLE WOMEN HAVE MULTIPLIED IN THE CHURCH AND MINISTRY TODAY.

NOTICEABLE PROBLEMS ASSOCIATED WITH SINGLE WOMEN MINISTERS

"Let not a widow be taken into the number under threescore years old, having been the wife of one man, Well reported of for good works; if she have brought up children, if she have lodged strangers, if she have washed the saints' feet, if she have relieved the afflicted, if she have diligently followed every good work. But the younger widows refuse: for when they have begun to wax wanton against Christ, they will marry; Having damnation, because they have cast off their first faith. And withal they learn to be idle, wandering about from house to house; and not only idle, but tattlers also and busybodies, speaking things which they ought not. I will therefore that the younger women marry, bear children, guide the house, give none occasion to the adversary to speak reproachfully. For some are already turned aside after Satan. If any man or woman that believeth have widows, let them relieve them, and let not the church be charged; that it may relieve them that are widows indeed."

- I TIM. 5:9-16

THERE HAD BEEN MANY PROBLEMS THAT HAVE EMANATED DUE TO THE UPSURGE OF SINGLE WOMEN IN MINISTRY TODAY. THESE PROBLEMS

121

REARED THEIR HEADS IN THE FIRST CENTURY CHURCH AND APOSTLE PAUL HAD TO ADDRESS THEM. SOME OF THEM ARE:

GETTING INVOLVED WITH MEN ONE WAY OR THE OTHER.

POLLUTING THE CHURCH THROUGH IMMORAL LIVING.

CAUSING TROUBLE WITH THEIR MOUTH AND LIFESTYLES.

NEGLECTING THEIR CHILDREN IN THE NAME OF MINISTRY.

DOMINEERING AND STUBBORN ATTITUDES.

BEING HARASSED BY MALE MEMBERS FOR GRATIFICATION.

MALE MEMBERS NOT REALLY SUPPORTING THEIR MINISTRY.

REFUSING TO MARRY DESPITE THE WEAKNESS OF THEIR FLESH.

If you find yourself as a single woman minister, then these are scriptural standards that you must uphold and live by,

THERE ARE CASES OF SINGLE WOMEN MINISTERS WHO TEMPT THEIR SENIOR PASTORS TO COMMIT SIN, SLEEPING WITH THEIR PERSONAL ASSISTANTS, HEAD PASTORS AND GENERALLY CONSTITUTING THEMSELVES INTO NUISANCE IN THE MINISTRY.

ACCEPTABLE STANDARDS FOR THE SINGLE WOMAN MINISTER

"And there was one Anna, a prophetess, the daughter of Phanuel, of the tribe of Aser: she was of a great age, and had lived with an husband seven years from her virginity; And she was a widow of about fourscore and four years, which departed not from the temple, but served God with fastings and prayers night and day. And she coming in that instant gave thanks likewise unto the Lord, and spake of him to all them that looked for redemption in Jerusalem."
- LUKE 2:36-38

IF YOU FIND YOURSELF AS A SINGLE WOMAN MINISTER, THEN THESE ARE SCRIPTURAL STANDARDS THAT YOU MUST UPHOLD AND LIVE BY, JUST AS PROPHETESS ANNA LIVED BY THEM.

1. BE SURE OF YOUR CALLING INTO CELIBACY:

IF GOD HAS CALLED YOU INTO CELIBACY, THEN HE WILL GIVE YOU THE GRACE TO OVERCOME THE FLESH EASILY. BUT IF HE HAS NOT CALLED YOU INTO CELIBACY, PRAY, GET MARRIED AND STAY MARRIED.

2. SETTLE YOUR MARITAL CHALLENGES:

IF YOU ARE LESS THAN 60 YEARS OLD, AND YOU HAVE NOT RECEIVED A CALLING INTO CELIBACY, YOU WILL HAVE TO PRAY THROUGH AND CONSULT MINISTRY ELDERS FOR GODLY SOLUTION TO YOUR MARITAL CHALLENGES. YOUR MARRIAGE IS CRUCIAL TO YOUR ACCEPTANCE AS A WOMAN MINISTER. AND YOU MUST MARRY OR RE-MARRY RIGHTLY.

3.   BE UNDER THE COVERING OF A MAN:

EVEN IF YOU ARE SINGLE FOR NOW, YOU MUST HAVE A MALE AUTHORITY IN YOUR LIFE AND MINISTRY. BE A WOMAN UNDER THE AUTHORITY OF A GODLY MAN OF GOD WHO CAN SPEAK INTO YOUR LIFE WITH NO STRINGS ATTACHED. DON'T BE THE ALL-IN-ALL.

4.   CELEBRATE YOUR SINGLENESS:

SINGLENESS DOESN'T NECESSARILY HAVE TO BE LONELINESS. LET IT BE TIME OF FELLOWSHIP AND DEEP COMMUNION WITH THE LORD. LIVE TO PLEASE THE LORD AND DRAW CLOSER TO HIM.

5.   WATCH YOUR RELATIONSHIPS

LIVE ABOVE BOARD AND REPROACH. RUN AWAY FROM EVERY APPEARANCE OF EVIL. DON'T WALK AT THE BRINK OF SIN. WATCH YOUR HEART AND WHO YOU RELATE WITH. RUN FROM WHAT WILL LEAD YOU TO SIN. DON'T MOVE WITH PEOPLE OF QUESTIONABLE CHARACTERS.

6.   GOSSIP THE GOSPEL:

RATHER THAN ENGAGE IN FRIVOLITIES AND VANITIES OF THIS LIFE, DEVOTE YOURSELF TO GOSSIPING THE GOSPEL AND WINNING SOULS FOR THE LORD.

MINISTERIAL ETHICS FOR FEMALE MINISTERS

I ONCE MET A FEMALE MINISTER IN A CONFERENCE AND SHE LATER INVITED ME TO HER CHURCH FOR MINISTRATION AND TRAINING OF HER WORKERS AND STAFF. BUT EACH TIME I LOOK AT HER, SOMETHING HAPPENS IN MY HEART. INITIALLY, I THOUGHT I HAD A PROBLEM, BUT SHE LATER PROVED THAT SHE IS A FLIRT. WHILE MINISTERING IN HER CHURCH ONE TIME, SHE STEPPED FORWARD TO PINCH MY CHEST IN THE NAME OF PICKING MY POCKET BALL PEN TO WRITE. I FELT UNCOMFORTABLE. SHE LATER GAVE ME A GIFT OF BOXER AND SINGLET AFTER A TRAINING PROGRAMME. I REFUSED TO WEAR THE BOXER. SHE LATER ASKED ME TO COME TO HER HOUSE IN THE AFTERNOON AND ON A PARTICULAR DAY IF I WANT TO PICK UP THE

MONEY FOR THE SALES OF OUR BOOK THAT WE LEFT IN HER CHURCH. I REFUSED AND FORGOT THE MONEY WITH HER TILL TODAY. THIS IS AN UNBECOMING BEHAVIOUR IN A FEMALE MINISTER. IT IS AGAINST MINISTERIAL ETHICS.

These things (Ethics) write I unto thee, hoping to come unto thee shortly: but if I tarry long, that thou mayest know how thou oughtest to behave thyself in the house of God, which is the church of the living God, the pillar and ground of the truth."

− I TIM. 3:14-15.

MINISTERIAL ETHICS ARE THE ACCEPTABLE BEHAVIOURAL STANDARD EXPECTED OF EVERY MINISTER. THEY ARE THE CODE OF CONDUCTS FOR EVERY MINISTER OF THE GOSPEL.

TODAY, MANY WOMEN MINISTERS AND MINISTERS' WIVES ARE DEFICIENT IN MINISTRY PRIMARILY BECAUSE THEY ARE DEFICIENT IN ETHICS.

MINISTERIAL ETHICS ARE TOO BROAD TO BE ADDRESSED COMPLETELY IN JUST ONE WAY AND THAT'S WHY WE SHALL GIVE CONSIDERATION TO SOME IMPORTANT ONES AS THEY RELATE TO VARIOUS SEGMENTS AND ISSUES OF MINISTRY.

IN RELATION TO RELATING WITH MEN

*   DON'T HAVE ANY PRIVATE DISCUSSION WITH

ANY MAN IN PRIVACY EXCEPT YOUR HUSBAND. ANY SECRET YOU CANNOT SHARE WITH YOUR HUSBAND WILL CAUSE YOU PROBLEM AND SHAME SOME DAY.

* BEWARE OF MENTORS AND FATHERS IN THE LORD WHO WANT TO TAKE ADVANTAGE OF YOU. SOME MENTORS HAVE BECOME TORMENTORS TO THEIR MENTOREES.

* IT IS ETHICALLY WRONG TO VISIT A MAN ALONE WITHOUT ANY ONE WITH YOU OR WITH THE MAN.

* IT IS ETHICALLY WRONG TO ALWAYS DISCUSS THE WEAKNESS OF YOUR HUSBAND WITH OTHER MEN OUTSIDE WHO CANNOT IN ANY WAY BE OF HELP TO YOU.

* NEVER INTRODUCE A MAN TO A WOMAN EXCEPT SHE IS A WORTHY MINISTER.

* IF YOU ARE A SINGLE MINISTER, NEVER INVITE A MAN TO YOUR HOUSE FOR PRIVATE DISCUSSION. WHAT YOU NEVER BARGAINED FOR MAY HAPPEN.

* BEWARE OF HANDSHAKE, HUGGING AND PECKING WITH MEN WHICH AROUSES LUST IN YOUR HEART.

* IT IS UNETHICAL TO DISCUSS ABOUT SENSITIVE AREAS OF YOUR BODY WITH THE OPPOSITE SEX.

IN RELATION TO PUBLIC APPEARANCE

* DRESS THE WAY YOU WANT TO BE ADDRESSED. YOU CANNOT DRESS LIKE JEZEBEL AND EXPECT TO BE ADDRESSED AS HOLY MARY. NEITHER

CAN YOU DRESS LIKE A MARKET WOMAN AND EXPECT TO BE ADDRESSED AS FIRST LADY. AND YOU CANNOT DRESS LIKE A LITTLE GIRL AND EXPECT TO BE ADDRESSED AS A REVEREND MOTHER.

* YOUR CLOTHING NEEDS NOT TO BE COSTLY, NEW, OR EXTRAVAGANT. LET IT BE SIMPLE AND NEAT.

* YOUR CLOTHING MUST BE CLEAN, NEAT, WELL GROOMED, AND WELL OCCASIONED.

"A VEST BESPATTER WITH GRAVY, HALF NAKED NOT REACHING BELOW THE ANKLE, A COAT SPRINKLED WITH HAIR AND DANDRUFF, AND WITH BUTTONS MISSING, A SOILED COLLAR, AND UNSHINED SHOES ARE ALL INDICATION OF LACK OF APPEARANCE ETHICS."

IN RELATION TO YOUR HEALTH AND WELL BEING

* CLEANINGNESS IS NEXT TO GODLINESS, AND HEALTH IS WEALTH, THEREFORE, BATH REGULARLY ON DAILY BASIS. USE PERFUME TO OVERCOME BODY ODOURS.

* MAKE ADEQUATE USE OF MOUTH WASHERS, DEODORANTS AND BRUSH YOUR TEETH AFTER EACH MEAL.

* EAT BALANCED DIET AND DISCIPLINE YOUR EATING HABIT.

* DRESS YOUR HAIR REGULARLY AND CULTIVATE

A BECOMING POSTURE.
* CONTROL EXCESS WEIGHT BY EXERCISING.

IN RELATION TO TABLE MANNER

1 WHEN EATING IN THE PUBLIC, PLACE YOUR NAPKIN ON YOUR LAP AS SOON AS YOU ARE SEATED AND PLACE IT AT THE RIGHT SIDE OF YOUR PLATE WHEN YOU FINISH EATING.

2 WHEN THE FOOD IS TOO HOT, NEVER SPIT IT OUT. QUENCH WITH WATER.

3 WHEN YOU COUGH AT THE TABLE. DO SO BEHIND THE HAND, UNLESS IT CANNOT BE STOPPED.

4 WHEN YOU BLOW YOUR NOSE, IF THE NOSE MUST BE BLOWN AT THE TABLE, IT SHOULD BE DONE AS QUICKLY AS POSSIBLE WITH THE HEAD TURNED AWAY FROM THE TABLE.

5 WHEN YOU FIND FOREIGN MATTER IN THE FOOD, YOU SHOULD REMOVE IT WITH THE THUMB AND FOREFINGER.

6 BEFORE YOU TAKE A DRINK OF WATER, ALWAYS USE YOUR NAPKIN TO WIPE YOUR MOUTH.

7 TAKE YOUR TIME TO EAT LEISURELY AND COMFORTABLY AND ENDEAVOUR TO KEEP PACE WITH OTHERS.

8 ALWAYS REMOVE YOUR SPOON FROM THE TEA CUP BEFORE YOU SIP.

9 SIT DOWN AND GET UP FROM THE LEFT SIDE OF YOUR CHAIR.

10 EAT FROM THE SIDE OF YOUR SPOON.

11   EAT WITH THANKFULNESS.

IN RELATION TO INVITATION FROM OTHER MINISTRY / MINISTER

1.   MAKE SURE YOU GET A LETTER OF INVITATION STATING THE DETAILS OF THE PROGRAMME, VENUE, TIME, THEME AND TOPIC.

2.   ALWAYS COMMIT IT TO GOD IN PRAYERS. IF AFTER PRAYERS, YOU FEEL THE INVITATION SHOULD NOT BE HONOURED, HUMBLY INFORM YOUR HOST.

3.   GET THE CONSENT AND APPROVAL OF YOUR HUSBAND. DON'T BE TOO BIG TO ASK FOR HIS CONSENT.

4.   GET TO THE PROGRAMME VENUE ON TIME. IT WILL GIVE YOU AMPLE TIME TO ACCLAMATISE AND DO AWAY WITH ANXIETY.

5.   SEE IT AS AN OPPORTUNITY AND NOT A PRIVILEDGE. THIS WILL ENABLE YOU TO BE APPRECIATIVE.

6.   KEEP TO THE STIPULATED TIME GIVEN TO YOU TO MINISTER. DON'T BE IN THE HABIT OF GOING BEYOND THE TIME ALLOTED TO YOU.

7   DON'T GIVE YOUR CONTACTS TO CHURCH MEMBERS EXCEPT THE HOST PASTOR GIVES HIS PERMISSION.

8   PREPARE YOURSELF VERY WELL, BY PRAYER, STUDYING AND MEDITATION.

BE A
DEBORAH

THE NAME DEBORAH IS FROM THE HEBREW WORD WHICH MEANS 'BEE'. LET US LOOK AT THE EXCEPTIONAL QUALITIES IN THE LIFE OF A BEE THAT MAKES IT SO UNIQUE:

1. EVERY BEE HAS SPIRITUAL SENSITIVITY AND ALERTNESS WHICH GIVES IT SPIRITUALITY AND ABILITY TO PRODUCE HONEY. THERE IS A MESSAGE OF GOD TO EVERY BEE THAT ONLY A BEING CAN ACCESS FOR EXPLOIT. BE SENSITIVE TO THE VOICE OF GOD FOR YOUR NEXT LEVEL OF EXPLOITS.

2. EVERY BEE KNOWS ITS PURPOSE OF CREATION AND FOCUSES ON THAT

131

PURPOSE. WHY ARE YOU HERE? WHAT IS YOUR PURPOSE OF BEING ALIVE? LET IT BE YOUR PRIMARY FOCUS AND FIGHT ALL DISTRACTIONS.

3.   EVERY BEE IS DILIGENT. BE DILIGENT TO STUDY, LISTEN, PRAY, RESEARCH AND MEDITATE.

4.   EVERY BEE MAKES A BUZZING NOISE WHEN FLYING. BE EXCITED ABOUT YOUR BEING AROUND AND JOIN OTHERS TO PRAISE GOD IN WOSHIP. MAKE A BUZZING VOICE OF PRAYER TO GOD.

5.   EVERY BEE ENJOYS CONNECTIONS AND RELATIONSHIP.
USE THE OPPORTUNITY YOU HAVE TO MAKE A HEALTHY CONNECTION AND RELATIONSHIP.

6.   EVERY BEE PROVIDES HONEY FOR OTHERS TO ENJOY. DETERMINE   TO MAKE A POSITIVE IMPACT ON YOUR WORLD, BY BEING A CONTRIBUTOR AND NOT ONLY A CONSUMER.

7.   EVERY BEE HAS ABILITY TO STING ITS ENEMY. BE EMPOWERED   TO FIGHT AND DEFEAT YOUR ENEMIES. YOU ARE A WINNER IN JESUS' NAME.

INTERNATIONAL CHURCH GROWTH MINISTRY

INTERNATIONAL CHURCH GROWTH MINISTRIES WAS FOUNDED IN 1994. THE VISION OF THE MINISTRY IS TO PROVIDE CURRENT AND RELIABLE CHURCH GROWTH PRINCIPLES IN AFRICAN CONTEXT TO LEADERS, PASTORS AND MINISTERS THAT WILL LEAD TO BETTER AND FASTER GROWTH OF THEIR CHURCHES.

WE DO THESE THROUGH BOOKS, MATERIALS, VCD AND AUDIO CASSETTES AT RELATIVELY LOW COST TO PEOPLE ENGAGED IN LEADING THE CHURCH.

WE EQUALLY ORGANISE SEMINARS AND CONFERENCES ON VARIOUS ASPECT OF CHURCH GROWTH AND HEALTH. WE ALSO ACCEPT INVITATIONS FROM CHURCHES TO

HELP ANALYSE THEM, MOTIVATE THEIR PEOPLE AND GENERALLY HELP THE GROWTH POTENTIALS OF CHURCHES.

SO FAR WE HAVE MINISTERED TO OVER 20,000 PASTORS AND CHRISTIAN WORKERS ACROSS MANY DENOMINATIONAL LINES AND INDEPENDENT CHURCHES. THE RESULTS HAVE BEEN TREMENDOUS AND THE TESTIMONIES HAVE BEEN WONDERFUL AND INTERESTING.

THE MINISTRY ALSO SAW THE NEED TO REALLY RAISE THE GROWTH CONSCIOUSNESS IN THE CONTINENT AND DECIDED TO PIONEER AN INSTITUTE ON CHURCH GROWTH. THE RESPONSE HAS BEEN OVERWHELMING AS SO MANY PASTORS, GENERAL OVERSEERS, AND CHURCH LEADERS HAVE ENROLLED TO LEARN MORE ABOUT HOW TO PRACTICALLY LEAD THEIR CHURCHES TO GROWTH. THE IMPACT OF THE INSTITUTE ON THESE PASTORS' LIVES HAVE STARTED MANIFESTING IN THE PHENOMENAL GROWTH OF THEIR CHURCHES AND EXPANSION OF

OTHER ICGM RESOURCES

I F YOU FOUND THIS BOOK TO BE USEFUL, YOU MAY BE INTERESTED IN SOME OF THE OTHER RESOURCES AVAILABLE FROM ICGM. LISTED BELOW ARE SOME OF OUR BOOKS AND RESOURCES:

BOOKS:
1. HOW TO SUPPORT AND STRENGTHEN YOUR PASTORS
2. LEADING FROM THE PULPIT
3. YOUR GROWTH IS YOUR FUTURE
4. THE SECRETS OF FINANCIALLY STRONG CHURCHES
5. CLOSING THE BACK DOOR OF YOUR CHURCHES
6. SPIRITUAL WARFARE AND CHURCH GROWTH
7. 40 STRATEGIC WAYS TO INCREASE CHURCH ATTENDANCE
8. SUPERNATURAL POWER, MIRACLES, SIGNS & WONDERS TODAY
9. OUR CHURCHES AND HIS CHURCH

10. STRATEGIC LIVING
11. LEADING YOUR CHURCH TO LASTING GROWTH
12. 22 DYNAMIC LAWS OF CHURCH GROWTH
13. STRATEGIC CHURCH PLANTING TODAY
14. THE PLACE OF ANOINTING AND ADMINISTRATION
15. THE IMPACT DRIVEN CHURCH
16. GROW THE PASTOR, GROW THE CHURCH
17. PERSONAL GROWTH TODAY
18. THE LOYAL ASSOCIATE
19. FRUITFUL AND FULFILLING MINISTRY TODAY
20. SEXUAL PURITY IN LEADERSHIP
21. GUEST MINISTERS TODAY
22. CHURCH CHANGE
23. 25 PILLARS OF CHURCH HEALTH
24. QUALITY AND QUANTITY GROWTH IN CHURCHES
25. HEALTHY LEADERS, HEALTHY CHURCHES
26. ANOINTING ALONE IS NOT ENOUGH
27. MONEY, MINISTERS & MINISTRY TODAY
28. 101 MINISTRY LESSONS
29. BRAKING THE BARRIERS OF SMALL, MIDDLE-SIZE & MEGA CHURCHES
30. HEALTHY HOMES
31. HOW TO FOLLOW WELL
32. THE RISE & FALL OF CHURCHES / MINISTRIES
33. TRUE SUCCESS, WEALTH AND PROSPERITY IN LIFE AND MINISTRY
34. PRAYER POWER FOR YOUR LIFE AND MINISTRY
35. 25 INDISPENSABLE QUALITIES FOR COMPETENT AND CREDIBLE MINISTER
36. THE KINGDOM OF GOD IS WITHIN YOU
37. YOUR CHURCH, YOUR COMMUNITY
38. THE CELL CHURCH

BOOKLETS
1. FAMILY GROWTH
2. PRAYER NUGGET
3. CHURCH GROWTH
4. FINANCIAL GROWTH
5. THE REAL MAN TODAY

RESOURCES:
A.   SPIRITUAL WARFARE FOR CHURCH GROWTH
B.   HELPING THE CLERGY - LEADING YOUR CHURCH TO GROWTH.
C.   PRACTICAL CHURCH PLANTING
D.   WINNING THE SOCIETY SEMINAR
E.   MOBILIZING THE LAITY
F.   WARFARE PRAYER FOR GROWTH
G.   CLOSING THE BACKDOOR OF THE CHURCH
H.   WOMEN MINISTRY IN CHURCH GROWTH
I.   STRATEGIC LEVEL PRAYER FOR BREAKTHROUGH
J.   SIGNS AND WONDERS FOR CHURCH GROWTH
K.   RESEARCH AND ANALYSING OF THE CHURCH
L.   HOW TO GROW A VIBRANT AND HEALTHY CHURCHES
M.   WHY CHURCHES LOSE MEMBERS
N.   EMPOWERING THE CHURCH FOR 21ST CENTURY
O.   HEALTHY LEADERSHIP FOR HEALTHY CHURCHES
P.   TOOLS FOR TREMENDOUS AND TRANSFORMING MINISTRY.
Q.   NEW WAVES OF GOD'S MOVE FOR END TIME HARVEST
R.   MAGNETIC, MULTIPLYING, MARKETABLE AND MAXIMUM IMPACT.
S.   BUILDING A BIGGER, BETTER AND BROADER CHURCH AND MANY OTHERS.

AUDIO TAPES, CD & VCD
1.   SPIRITUAL WARFARE SERIES
2.   EFFECTIVE MINISTERS SERIES
3.   WOMEN MINISTRY SERIES
4.   CLOSING THE BACKDOOR SERIES
5.   WARFARE PRAYER SERIES
6.   STRATEGIC LEVEL PRAYER SERIES
7.   CHURCH PLANTING SERIES
8.   HEALTHY CHURCH SERIES.

JOURNAL:

Sharpen your
Ministry Skills
and lead your church/// or ministry to the next level with

Books and Resources
from
Dr. Bola Akin-John

Int'l Church Growth Ministries

h o l d s

Pastor's Wives
and
Women
Ministers Conference

EVERY APPRIL

Pray, plan & prepare to attend

International
Church GROWTH
& LEADERSHIP
Conference

Every 3rd Week of February
& Last Week of Aug./Sept.

Two unique conferences for today's pastors, Bishops, Evangelists, Leaders, Minister

Dr. Francis Bola
AKIN-JOHN

* STARTED MINISTRY IN 1988.
* PASTORED FIVE DENOMINATIONAL CHURCHES IN THE SPACE OF 8 YEARS.
* STARTED CHURCH GROWTH MINISTRY IN 1994 AFTER HEARING GOD SAID "GO AND STRENGTHEN PASTORS AND SUPPORT CHURCHES TO GROW AND BE HEALTHY".
* HAS HELD HUNDREDS OF CONFERENCES ACROSS NIGERIA, AFRICA AND EUROPE WITH COMBINED ATTENDANCE OF MANY THOUSANDS OF CHURCH LEADERS.
* HAS WRITTEN OVER 35 BOOKS THAT HAS SOLD THOUSANDS OF COPIES SUCH AS 'GROW THE PASTOR, GROW THE CHURCH', 'THE IMPACT-DRIVEN CHURCH', AND '22 DYNAMIC LAWS OF CHURCH GROWTH'.
* FOUNDED INTERNATIONAL INSTITUTE OF CHURCH GROWTH THAT HAS TRAINED OVER 5,000 PASTORS AND LEADERS WITH ATTENDANT GROWTH TESTIMONIES.
* HAS WRITTEN AND PRODUCED HUNDREDS OF MATERIALS ON VARIOUS ASPECTS OF CHURCH GROWTH, LEADERSHIP AND HEALTH THAT IS BEING USED BY THOUSANDS OF CHURCH LEADERS.

143

Made in the USA
Coppell, TX
05 October 2021